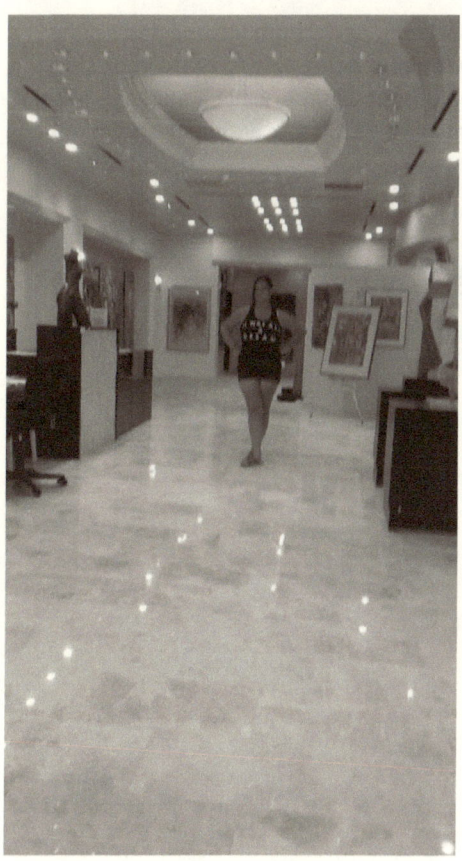

YEAR 2017,

It has a been a year since the dream of owning my own Art gallery and workshop has grown.

This is a gallery in Sarasota, FL, and it is the type of gallery I would like to see myself in and hope you do too in your journey has becomming your own artist.

Being a talented artist isn't about fame, perfection, income and selling techniques, being a true painter is about being able to share your story within you work and make it personal at all time. Have a message to send out and enjoy every minute you spend painting, creating or dreaming!

Dream Big and some day you ll have this gallery of your dream!

My digital mix up work of mix up expressionist artist.

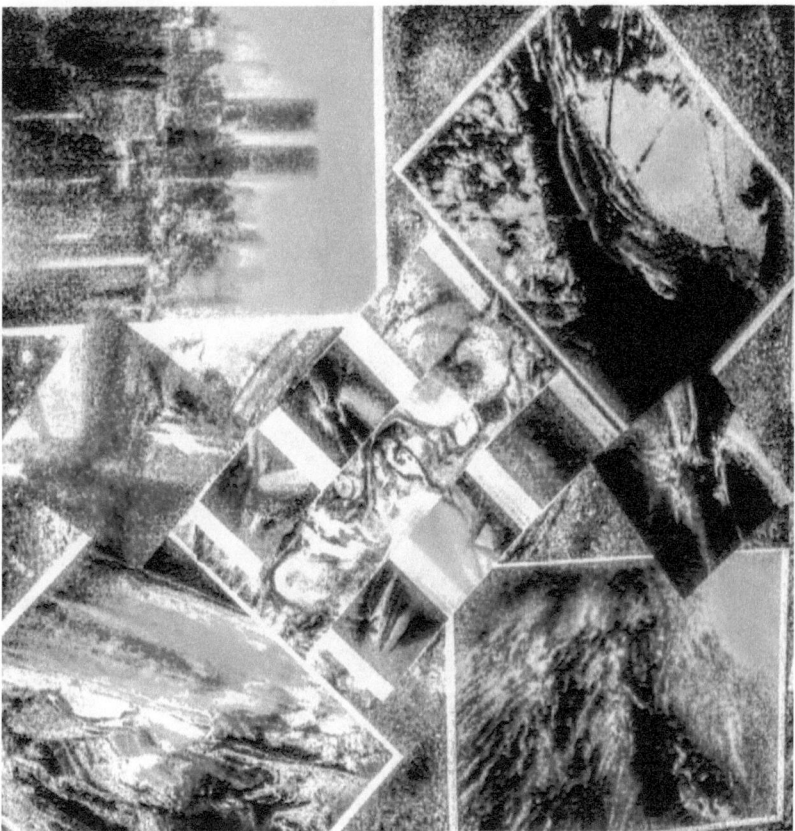

This was a way to capture a few artist with the same style into a different composition that will bring art technology into a light somehow.

This is the logo i used when creating my company " Vcreativeart16 " Stand for:

 Vanessa creative art in year 2016, because that's when i finally decided to stop being afraid of the competition and this outside world judgement and concretize my deep inner need to fullfill my talents.

I started totally online, 24/7 there was nobody to meet, to see or to work with, i picked up a few contest in a few state and various art group and ask if anyone wanted to join my new venture with no promise but in the goal off bringing love, joy, creativity to lives and bring peace to a world in distress.

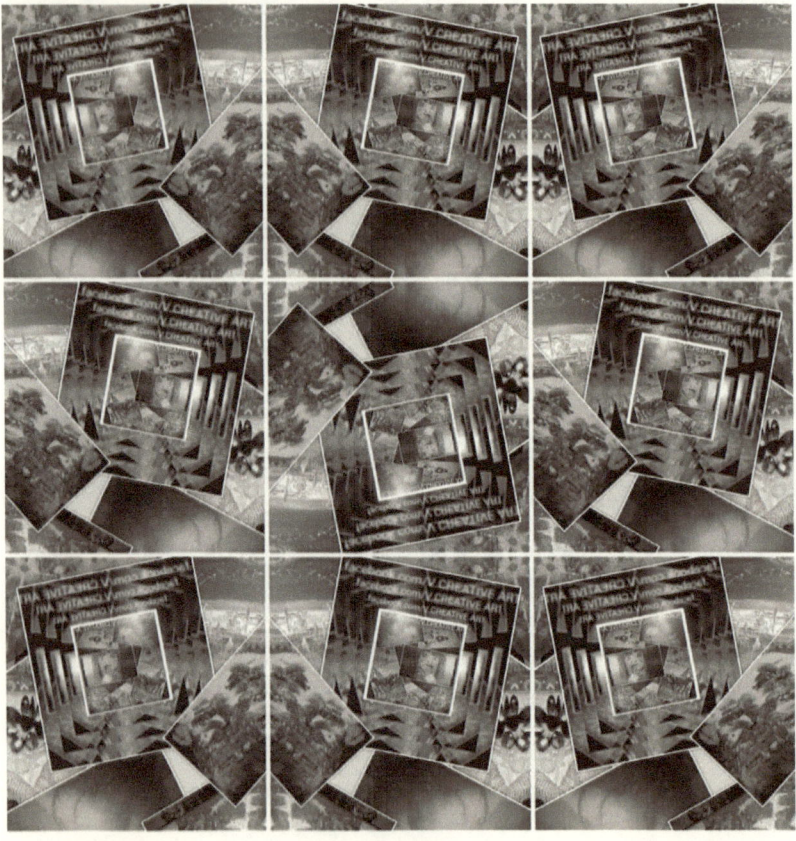

I called this" the walking feet" I used one of my acrylic very bright redish painting and used a light blurry pink background to gave it a spatial effect.

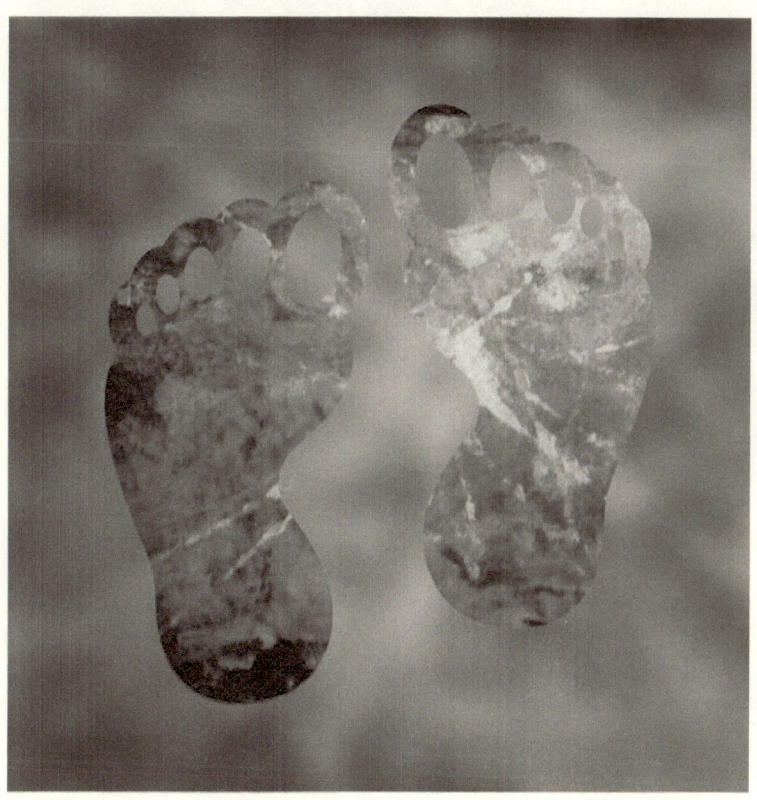

This i was very proud and recorded video to describe it
:https://www.facebook.com/VcreativeArt16/videos/1990699214490185/ along with other
paintings.

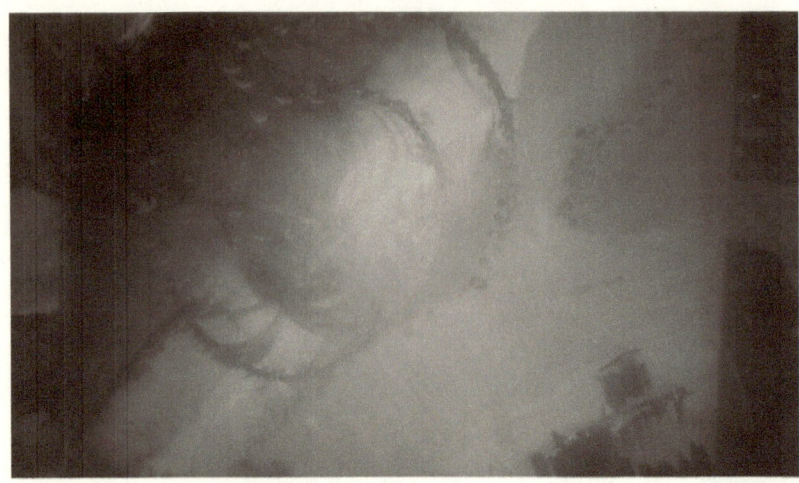

This is my fellow artist " Matthew Evans" a well establish impressionist painter, i feel in love with his landscape and we have been promoting for eachother and motivating others.

Here is a video i made for him on his present work:
https://www.facebook.com/VcreativeArt16/videos/2087321184827987/

He won award art gallery contest numerous times and work with Art therapy and different causes and disability high school in this UK.

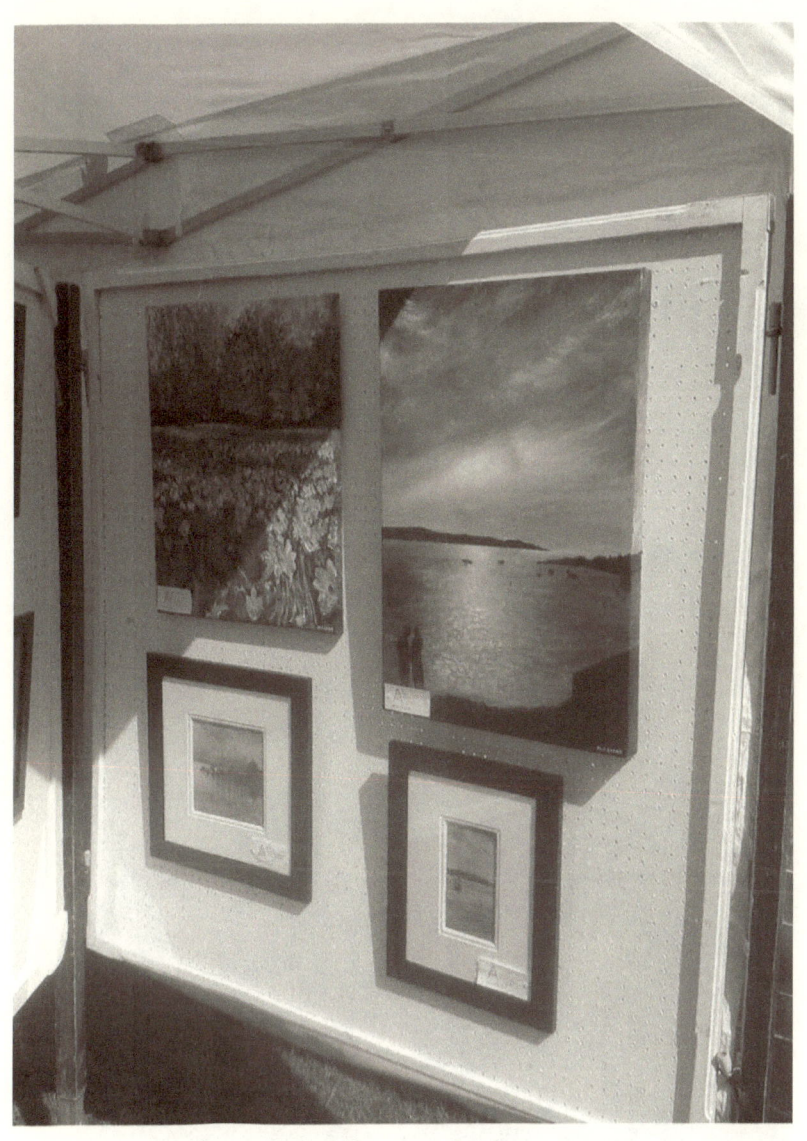

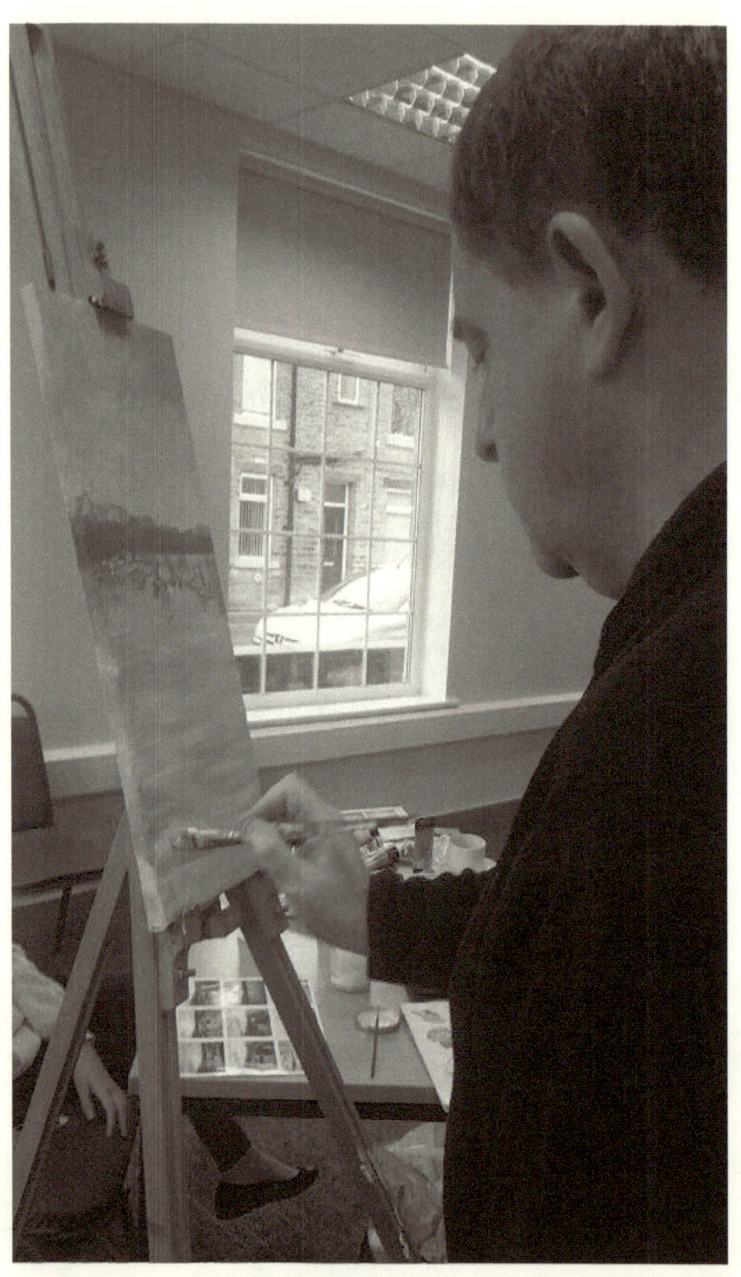

Here is the first video we made to combine our work, Matthew was the first Co-Artist to join Vcreativeart16 by the way in August 2016.

https://www.facebook.com/VcreativeArt16/videos/1942591025967671/

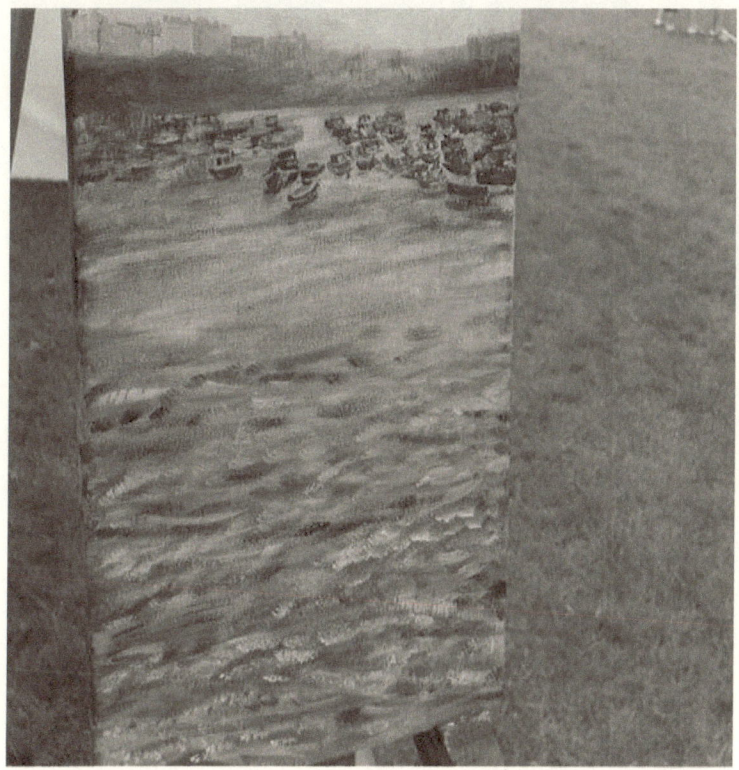

This was my first attempt to reenter into this impressionism world and use waterfall and sunset has references.

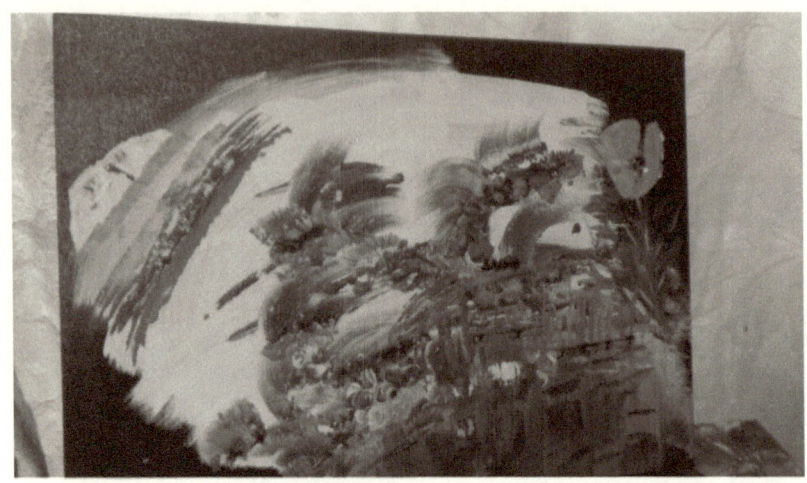

This spiral took me a few hours to create i used a lot of thick oil and a very small amount of acrylic or water. I wanted to bring a thunder effect of blurry and windy atmosphere.

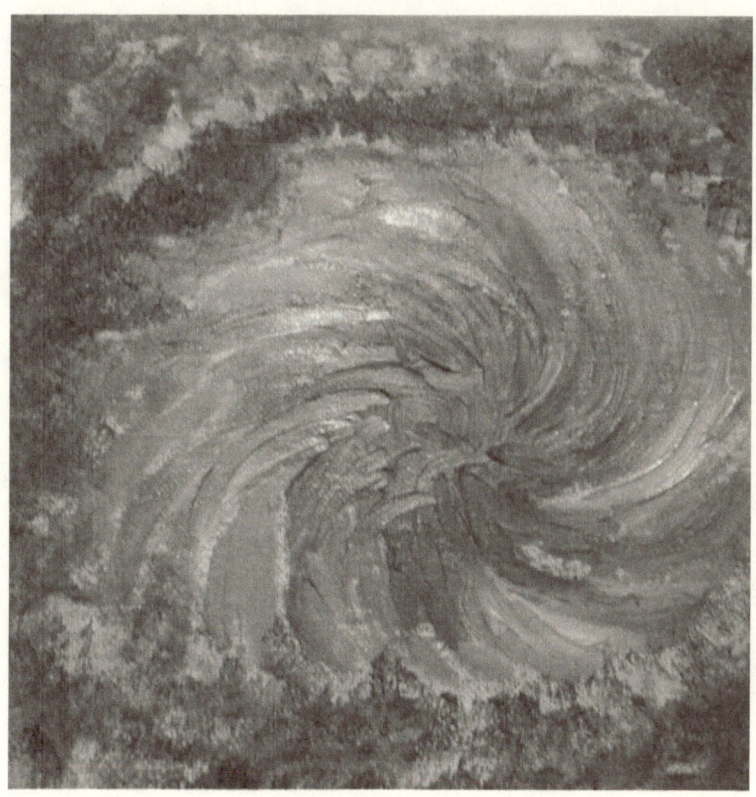

This is a very old sunset by this atlantic ocean, i created in 2000, showing you this to show you
that everyone has to start somewhere and that practice and knowledge with collaboration
and new techniques devellop over this years wil allow you to get exactly where you need to
go.

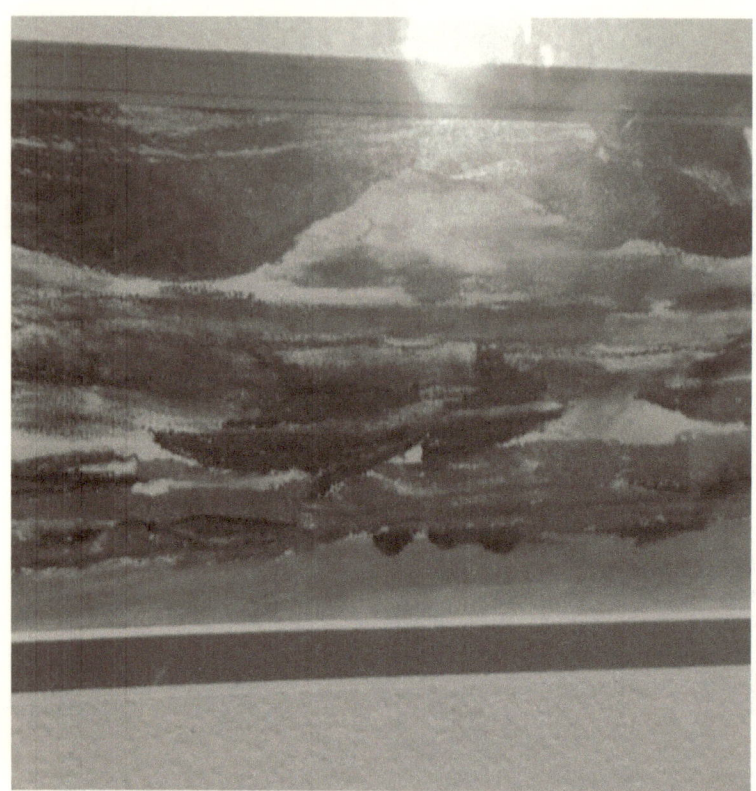

In year 2001, i was playing with pastel and crayons and i had to make this for a newspaper article to advertise a new coffee shop on Anna Maria Island, FL. I was in this hidden then but during that year i sold my first painting to our business owner neighboor who work has a architect and i was was so pleased that he would love my work, i didnt take picture back then if anything, neither make copies, it was a desert showing with tiny stone rocks that i design one by one and took over 8 hours to do. This day was a day that made you think" I knew i had talent" i will never stop!'.

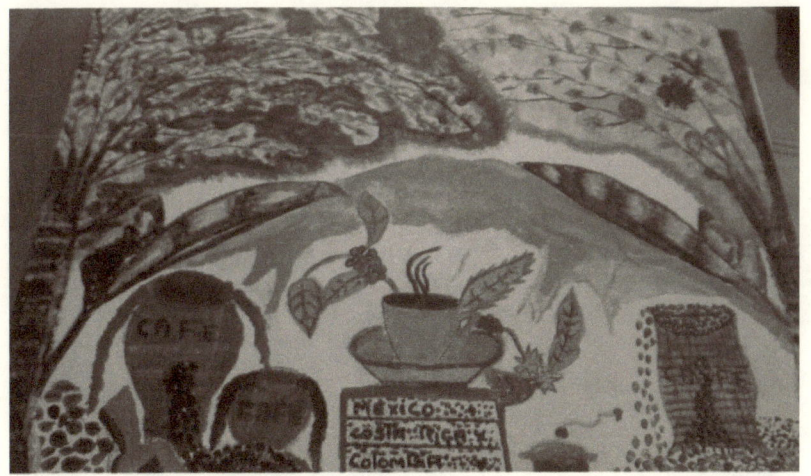

One of Matthew fantastic sunset!!!

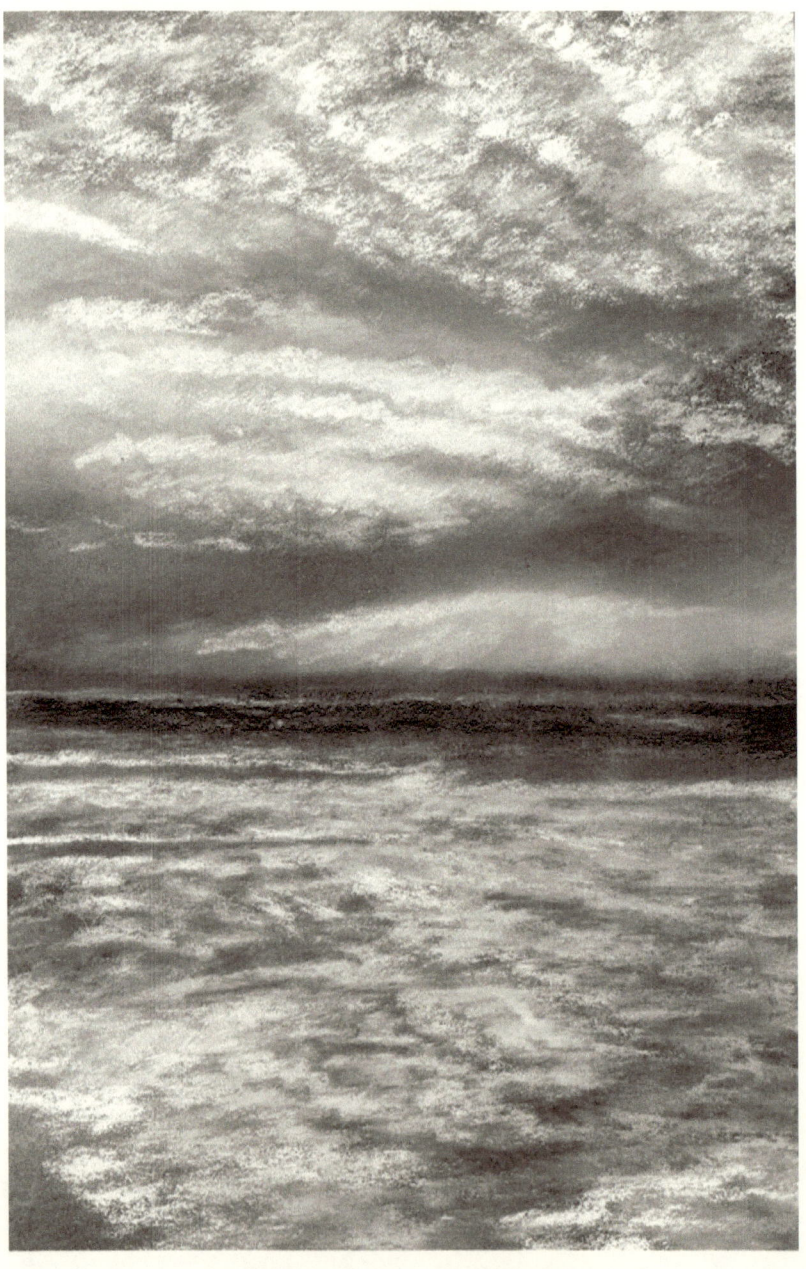

I spent a lot of time figuring out which logo i should use, so here I was playing with photoshop and digital enhancement.

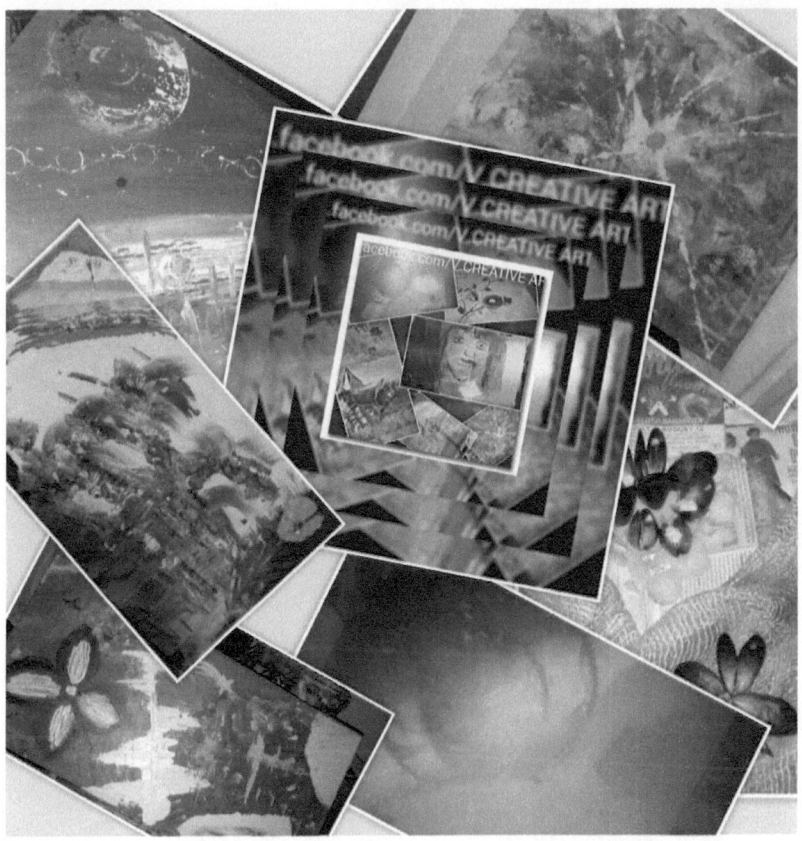

My little birdy was taking a flight through a mirror! Conditionning the transparency of double effect by lightning.

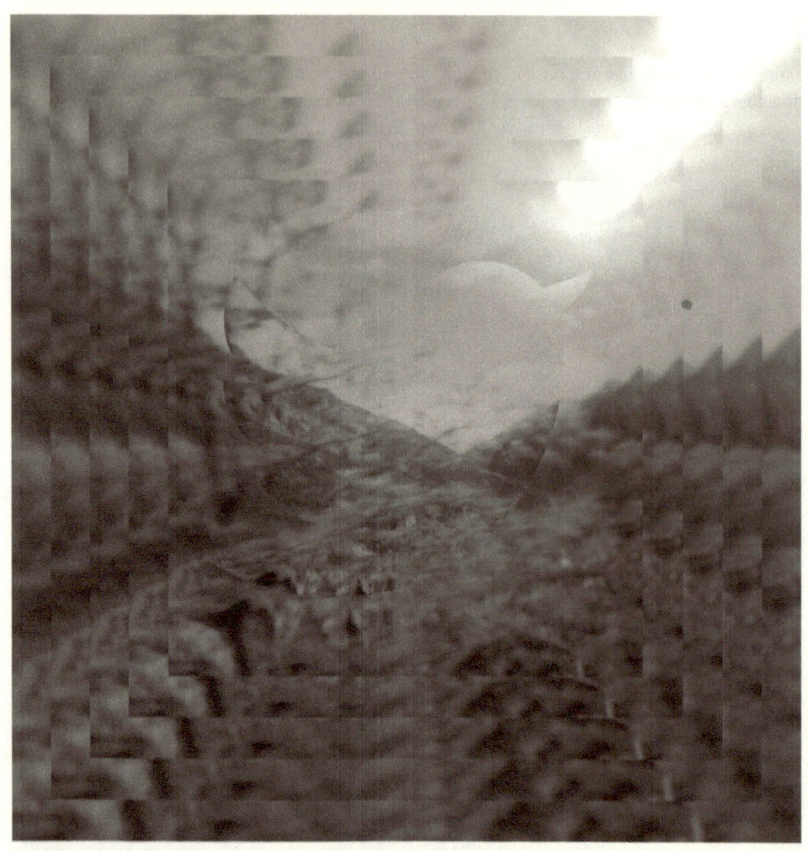

Matthew Evans " Impressionist" content

Watch how he capture this gentle waves and a peacefull soon to be dark night.

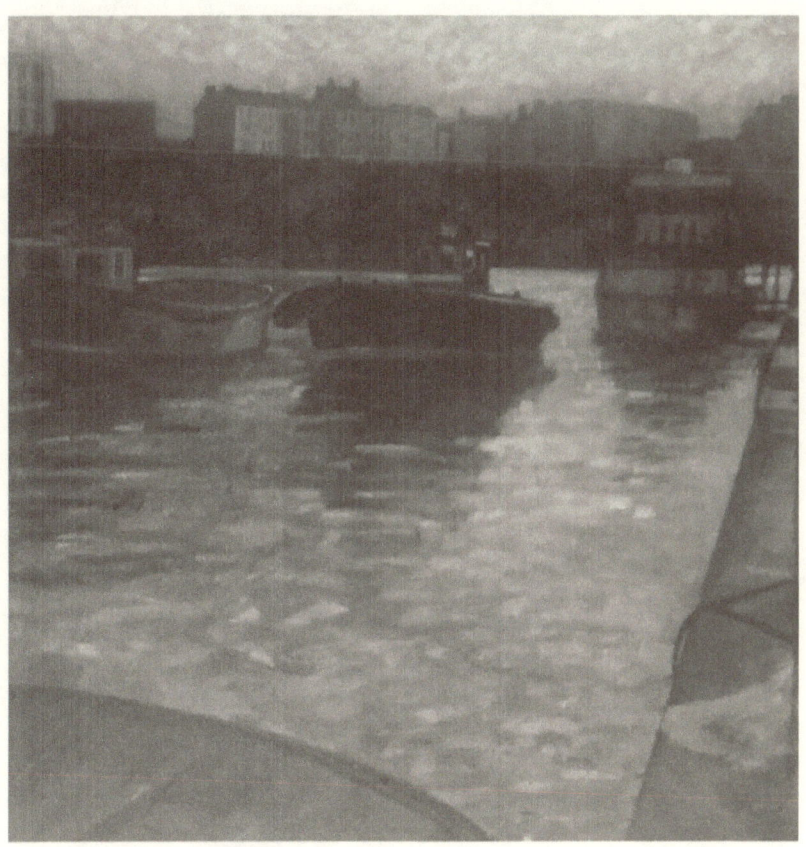

Playing into water paint and glowing paint for a fun kids art effect. This was made in this intention of designing a children book.

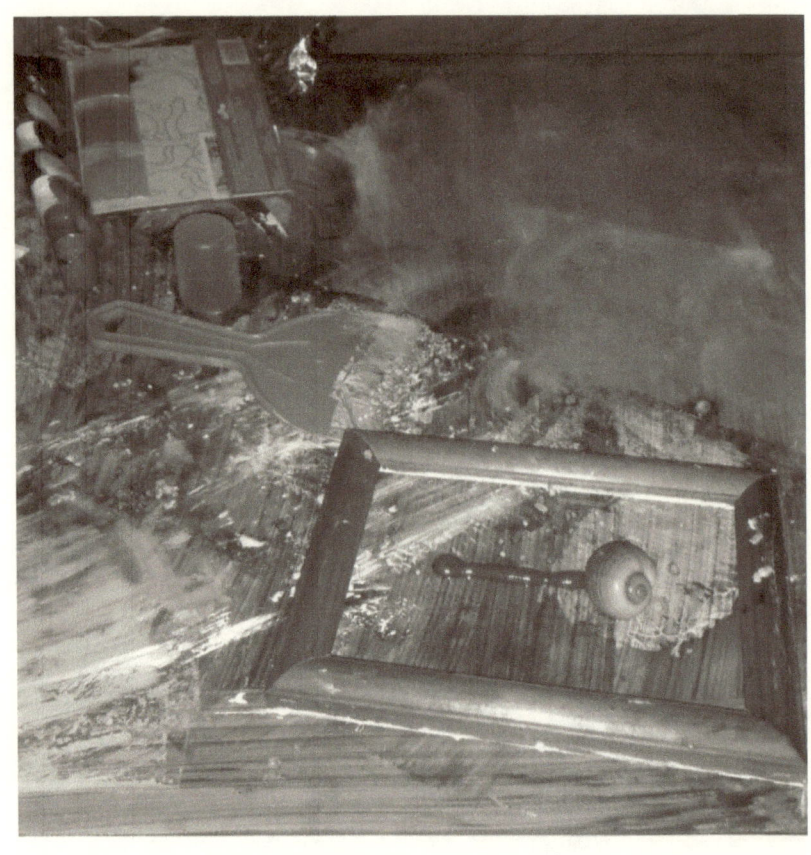

Reading through color and lightning effect instruction book i try to make my own capture bu adding row material into this landscape

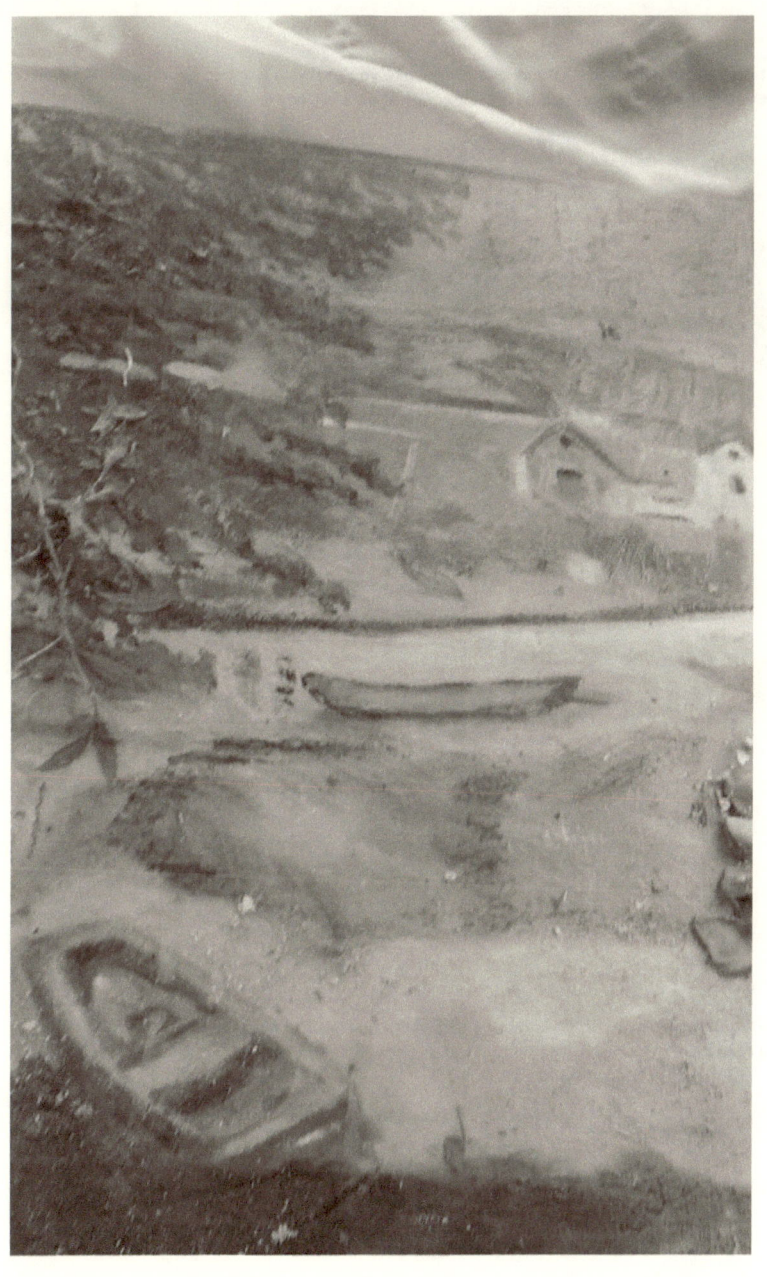

Emotion, Emotion!!!! when you in love or feel like you are! you want to express it and this is what you seing here! the result of my imagination on a brighty day!

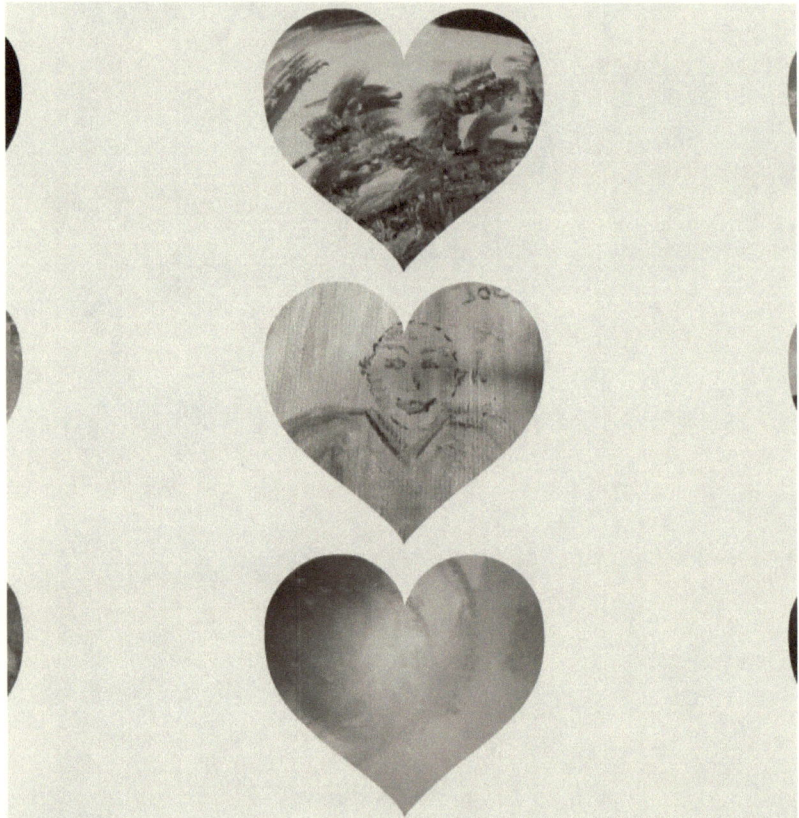

This is me a week later!!!! devasted, heartbroken. I even used a carton board to capture this state of unpleasant taught coming to mind.

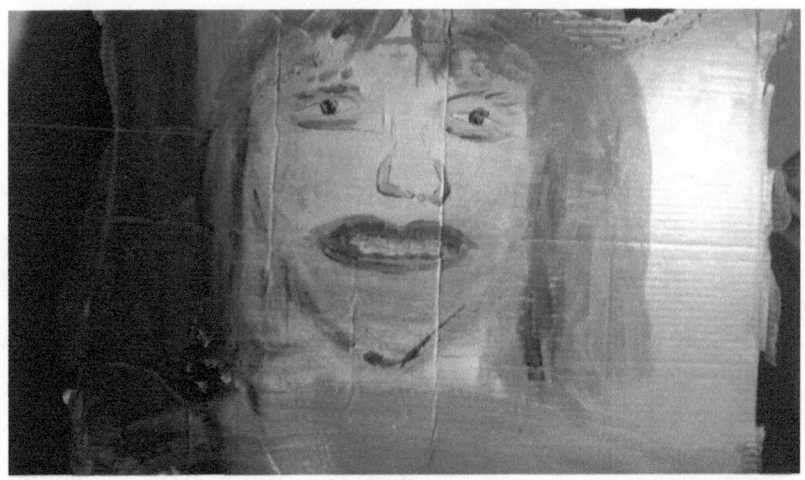

This love representation and dance culture painting is inspired by this ballerina and romantic encounters of this 18th century.

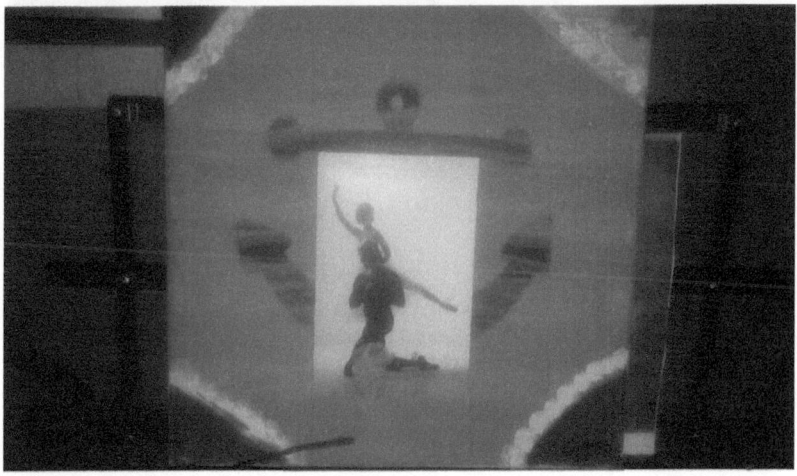

This is one of Matthew Evans signature, Flowers in the wild in every places.

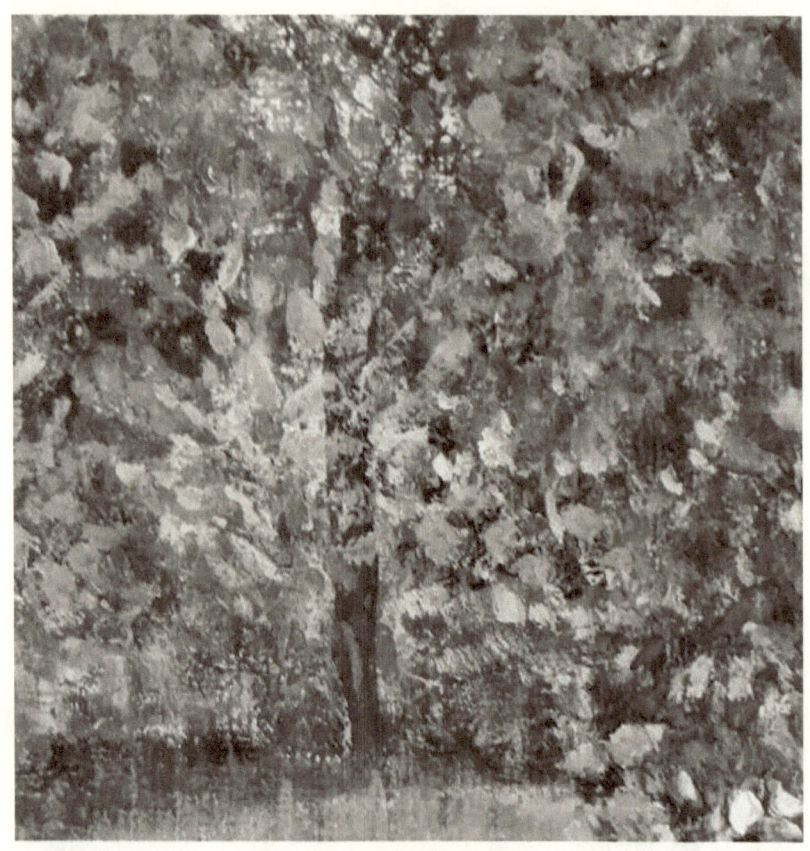

This is the work of water reflection style using only one color and simple paper.

Result: it gave you a simple flow of the water passing thru.

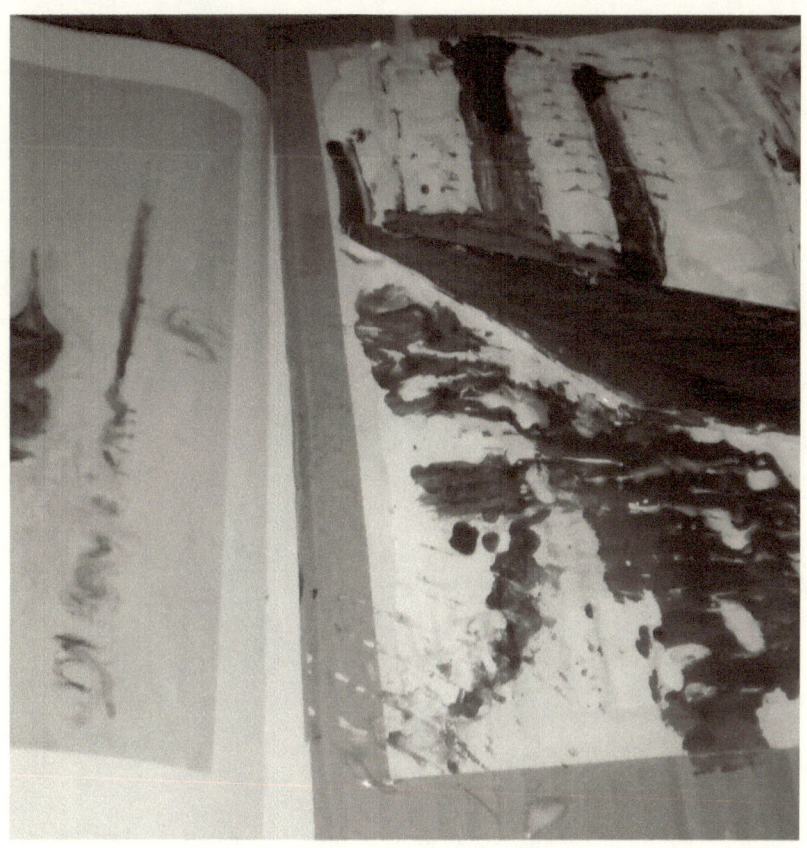

This is my representation of the women declaration of independance!

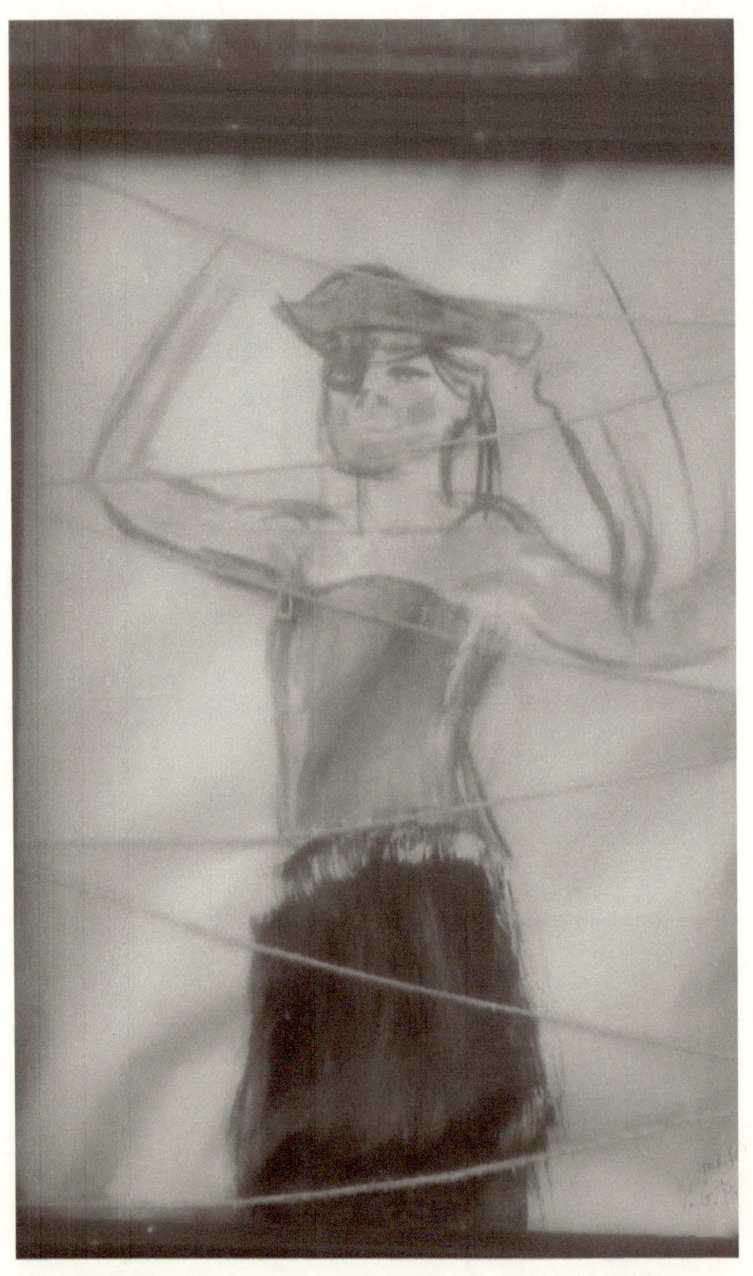

Those painintg are the work of all this co-artist who came to be part of " Vcreativeart16"

https://www.facebook.com/VcreativeArt16/videos/2043074625919310/

https://www.facebook.com/VcreativeArt16/videos/2046952768864829/

https://www.facebook.com/VcreativeArt16/videos/2109960142564091/

https://www.facebook.com/VcreativeArt16/videos/2111822669044505/

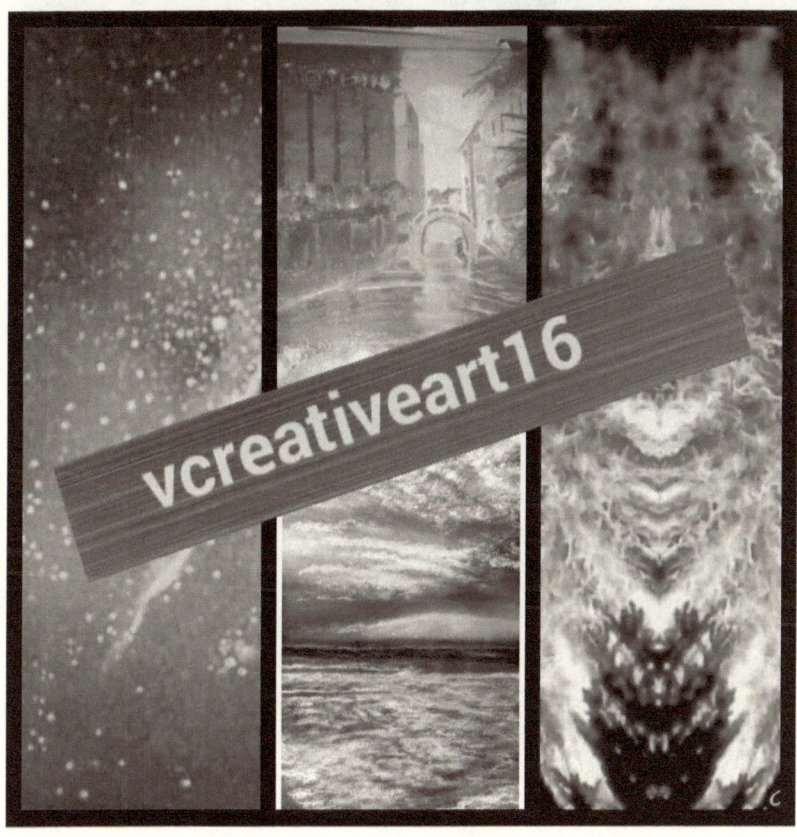

https://www.facebook.com/VcreativeArt16/videos/2040110169549089/

My fabulous symbol of love

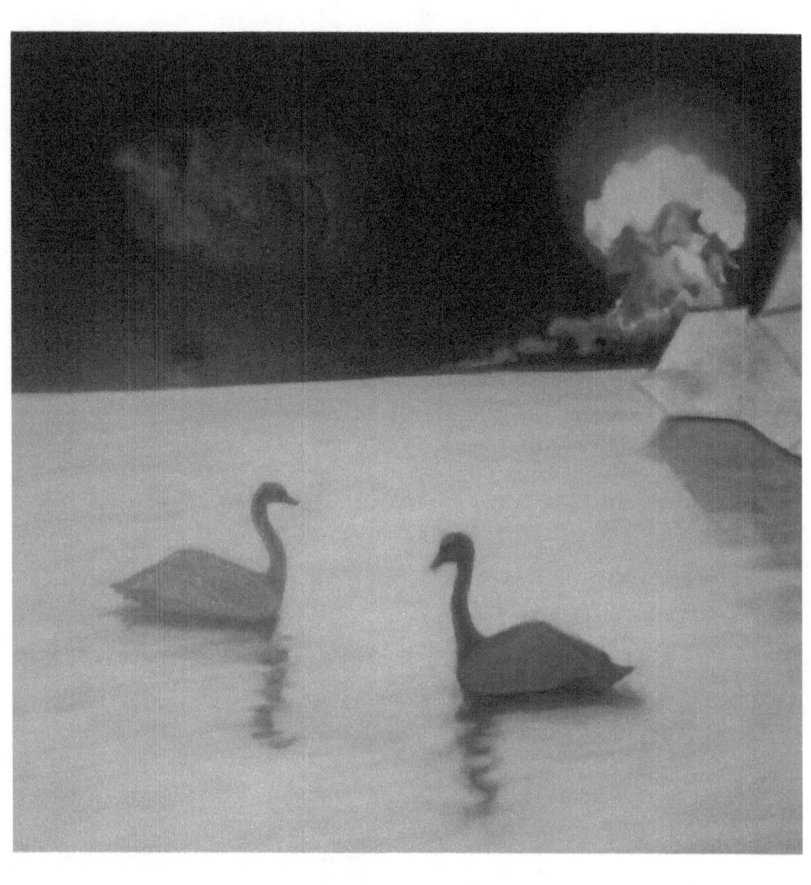

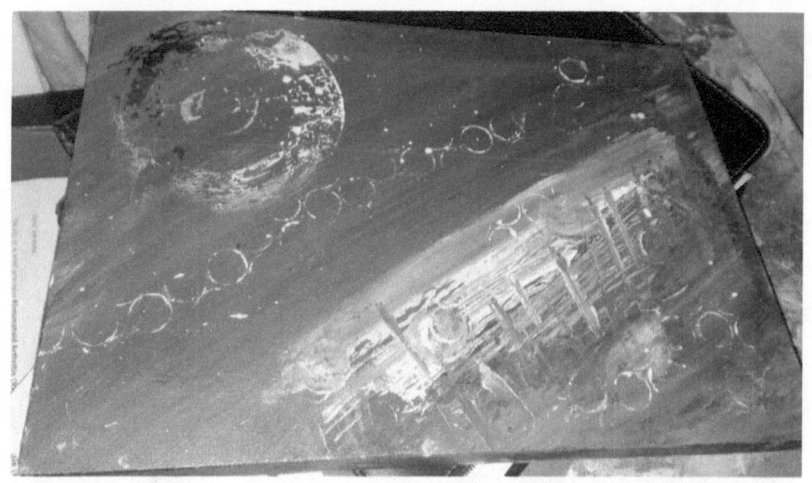

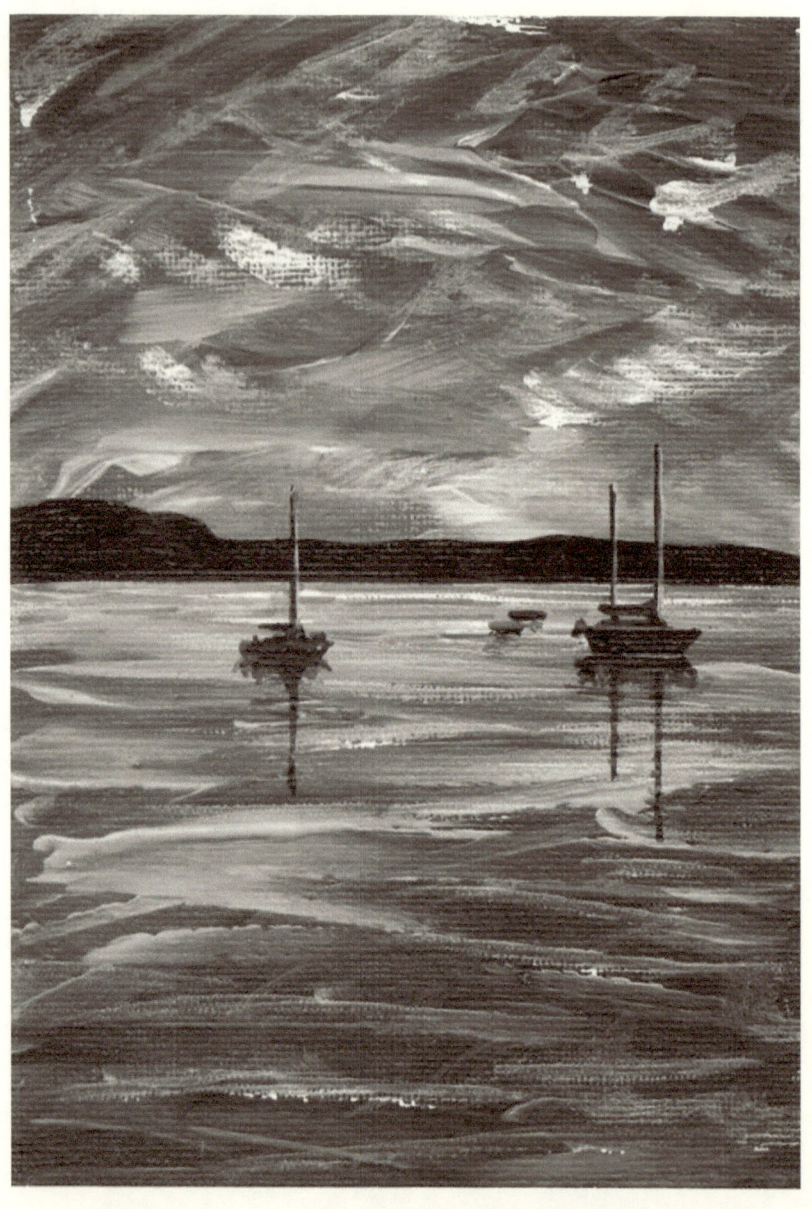

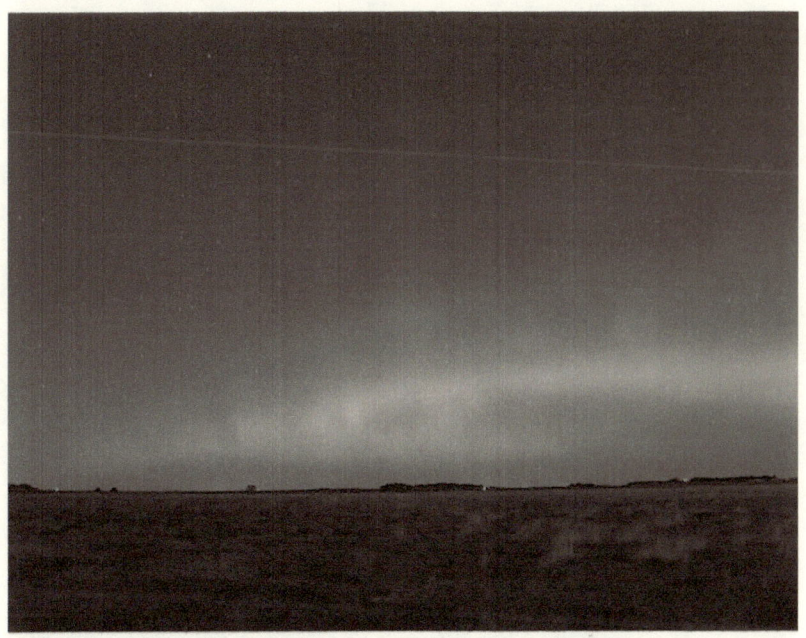

" La clairiere" I try to recopy the mannet painting of impressionism using my own color

This was hanging at " Manatee central library of Bradenton FL" for almost a year in 2016

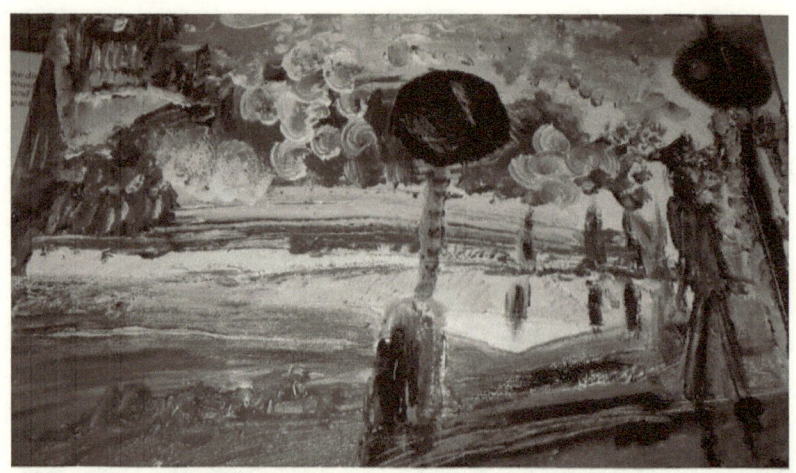

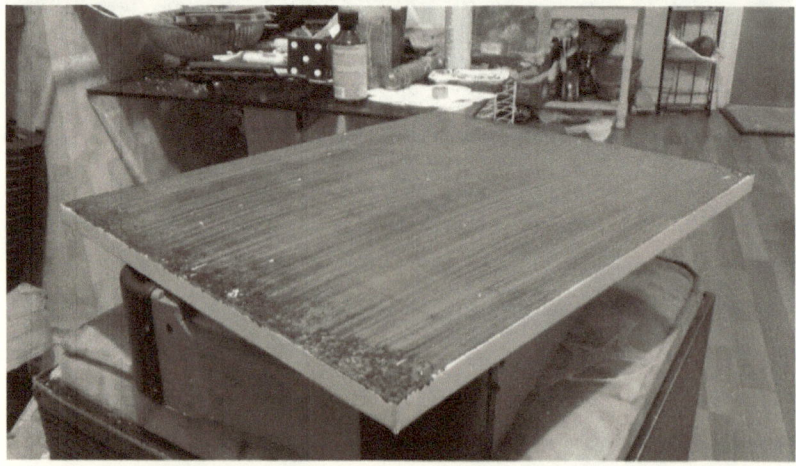

Painting is a lot of fun but once in a while i enjoy getting into digital photography and simple one on on photography and use my capture to enter many local nature contest yearly.

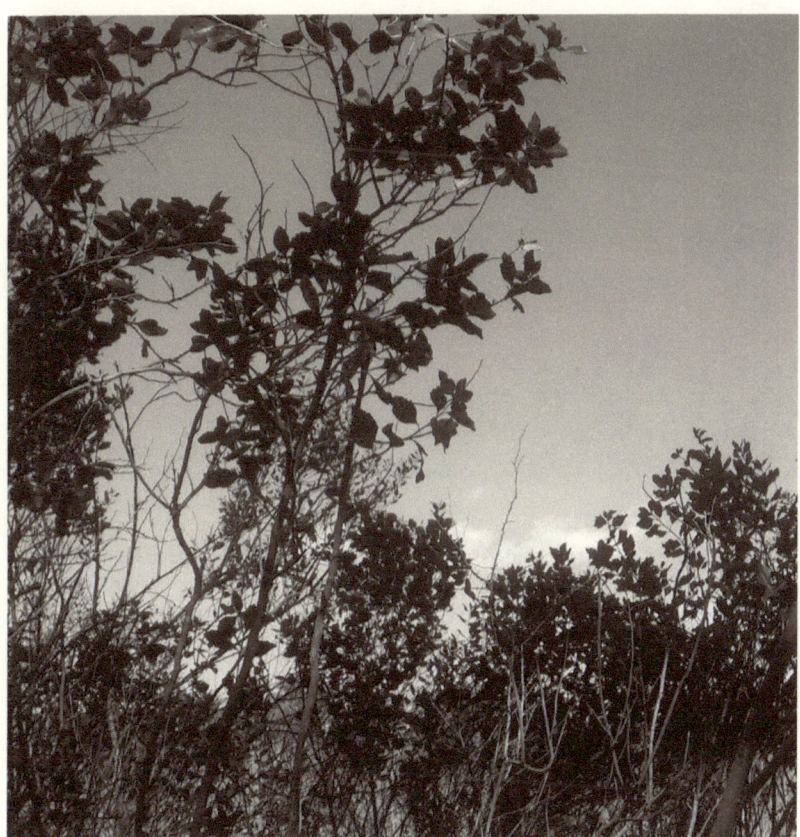

Description:

I wanted to go beyound this reflect light of the rainbow and natural sunlight by gaving a protusion effect has a abstract painter sometime you will want to swim inside your work and see what others can't see, so i immagined being in a jungle in Australia or in this Rain forrest and after a long day of hiking i find this tiny little waterfall surrounded by purple, yellow, red, pink wild plants and flowers creating a magnificient view and with the tiredness and the dehydration endured under the heat, my vision was perceived in a blurry vision.

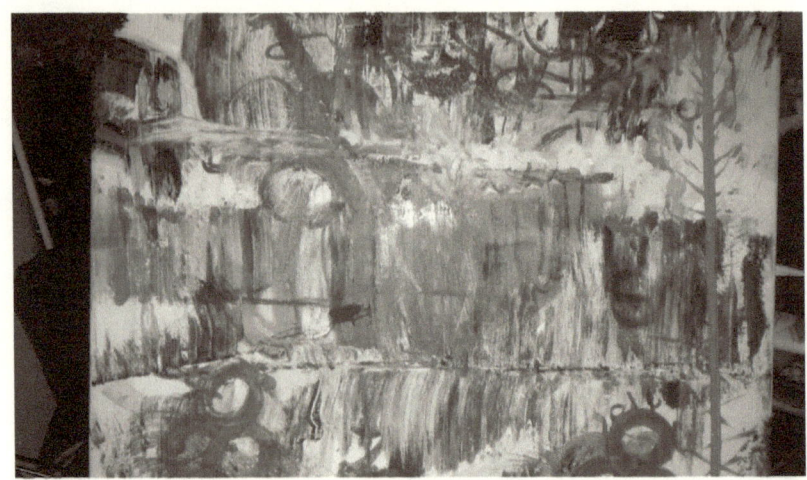

For this palm tree the story behind it is: I wanted to learn how to create cloud from watching professional do it and i used a little van gogh inspiration and added a country flair, has palm tree planted in a old farm in a sunny desert.

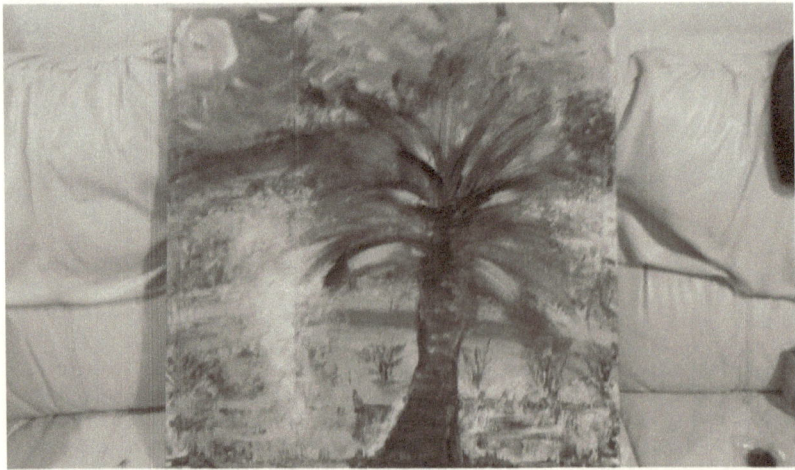

This came about working on a digital project contest to come up with a cover poster for a trance music company.

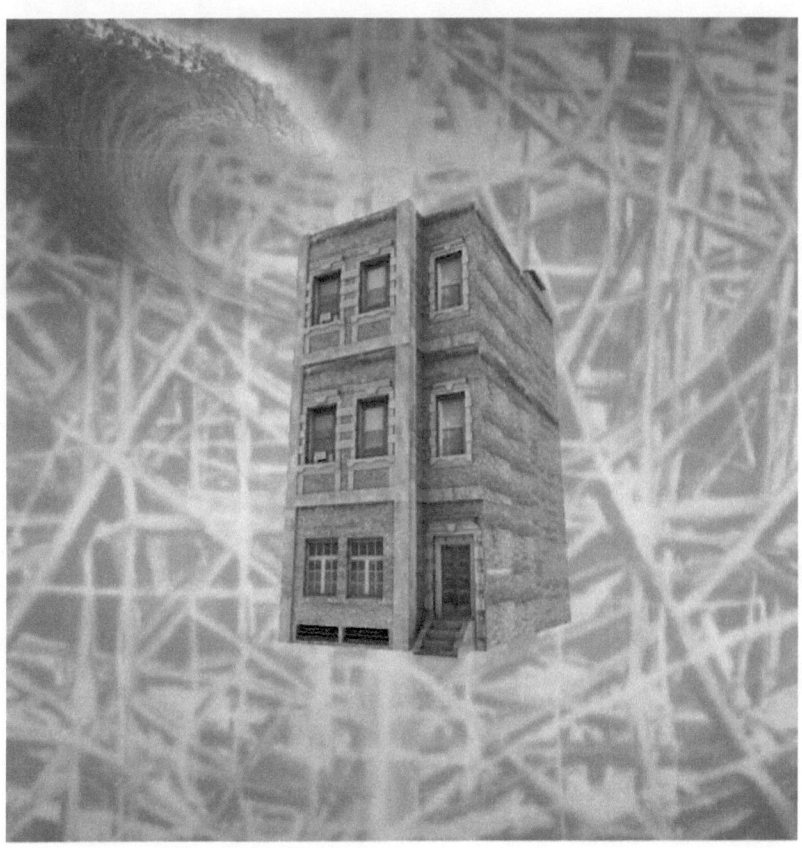

I felt inspired by thr product of love and romance combine, i wanted to capture the feeling of love by color flashing.

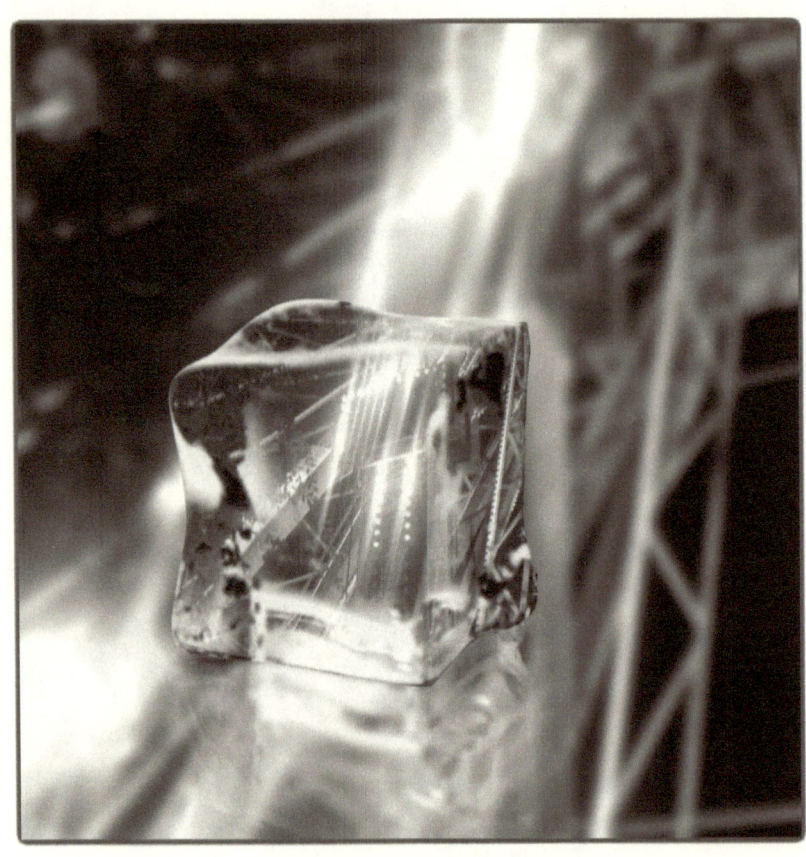

This is a image of how to paint the sunlight rays use for my lectures and demonstration

https://www.facebook.com/VcreativeArt16/videos/2131801767046595/

https://www.facebook.com/VcreativeArt16/videos/2087745338118905/

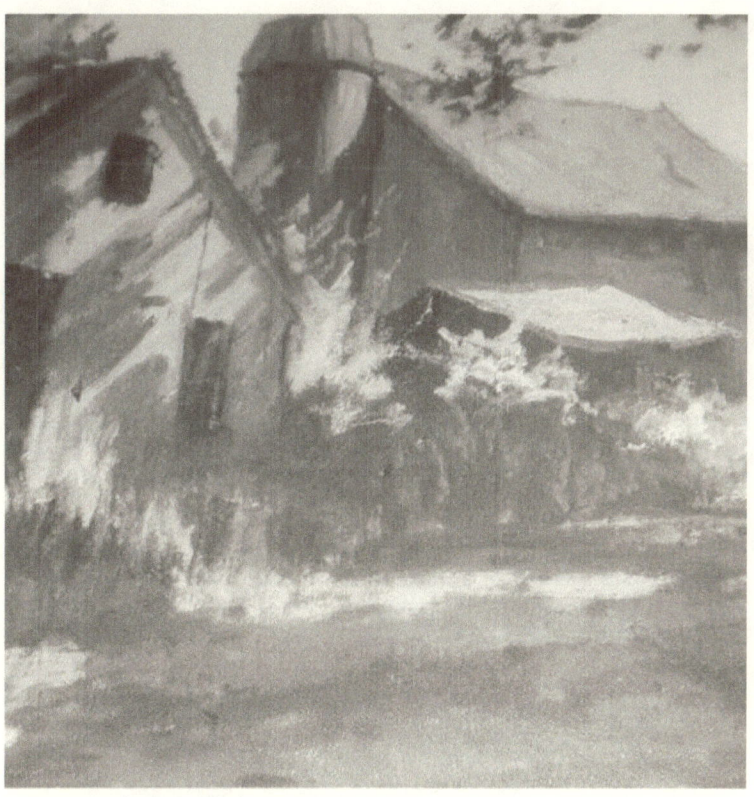

Description: I m very proud of this one, i used watercolor paint and a large white poster paper and it came out to look pretty good, i wanted to feel like the heat was so intense that you could see behind this original color of nature earth and have a sight of a fairy tale feel.

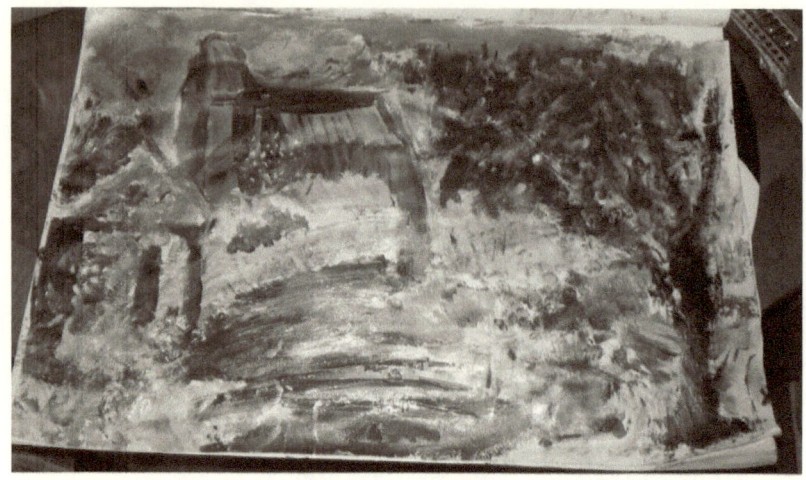

For this i was using a very cool app for a few month call " mobile artist" very easy to use and can convert any picture into fameous impressionist painter stryle, on top of converting my original picture i ll use my camera future to enhance this image.

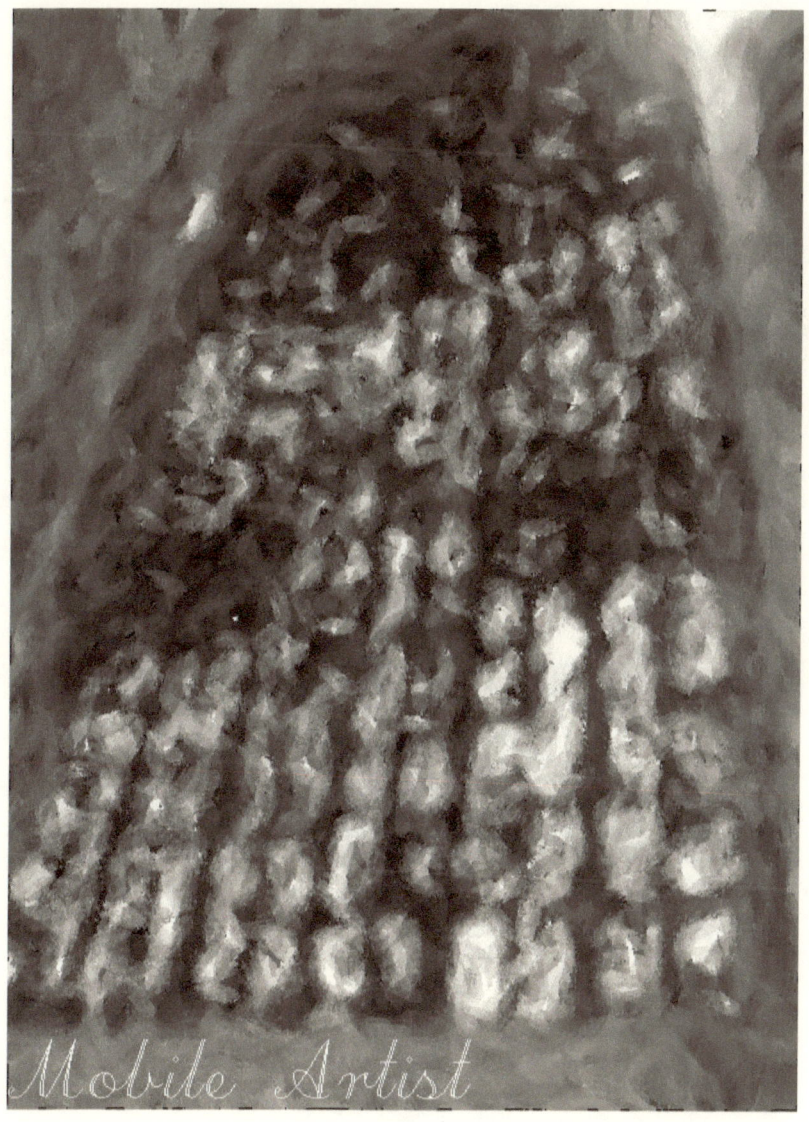

This i made after being inspired by some true technology paranormal and trance 3-d software

I still have a long way to go but i have all i need now and will learn to combine my art with 3-d imaging.

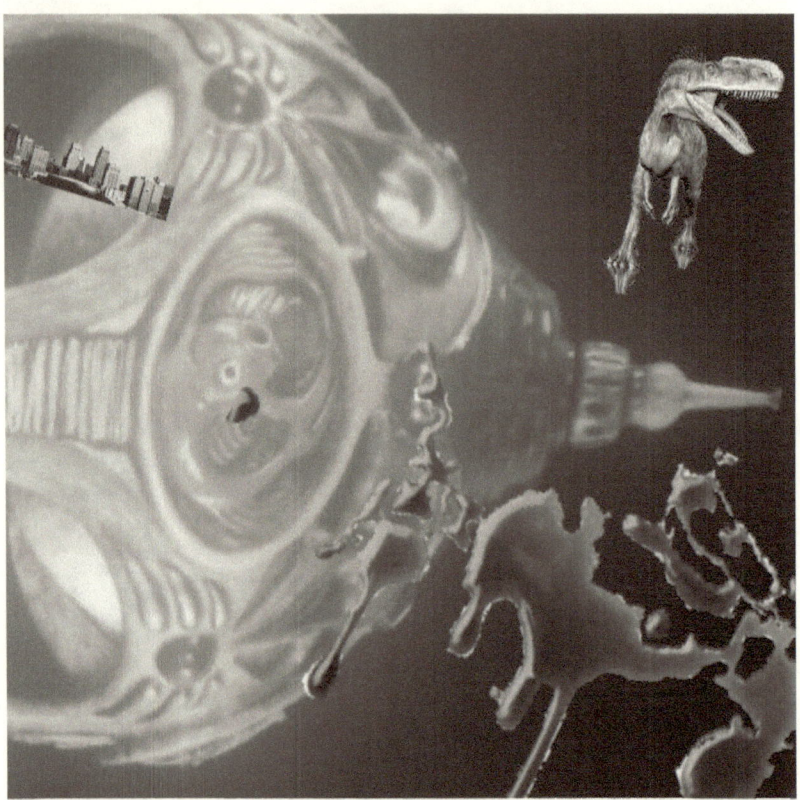

This is a typical abstract painting, very detailed and meaningful.

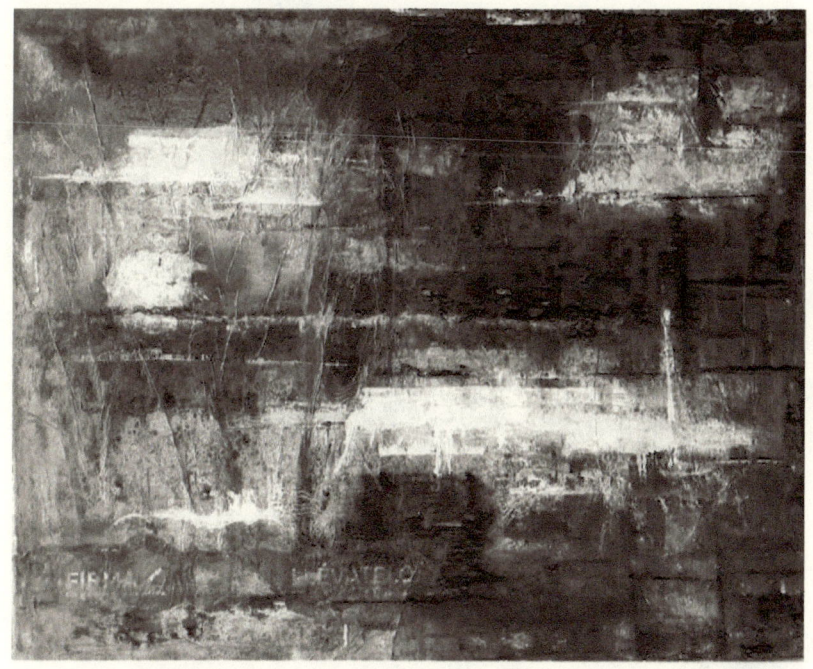

This is a oldie! Before i regained my confidence has a painter i still didn't believe in my art but was trying really hard, there a difference between having confidence in what you do and believing in what you create, once you truly find your mystery clue missing you can regain your inspiration and establish your true authentuc flair has a artist.

Every artist have their own style even if sometimes it';s hard to differentiate they isn't one single same artist in the world and if you do find them that's because they are phonies or thieves.

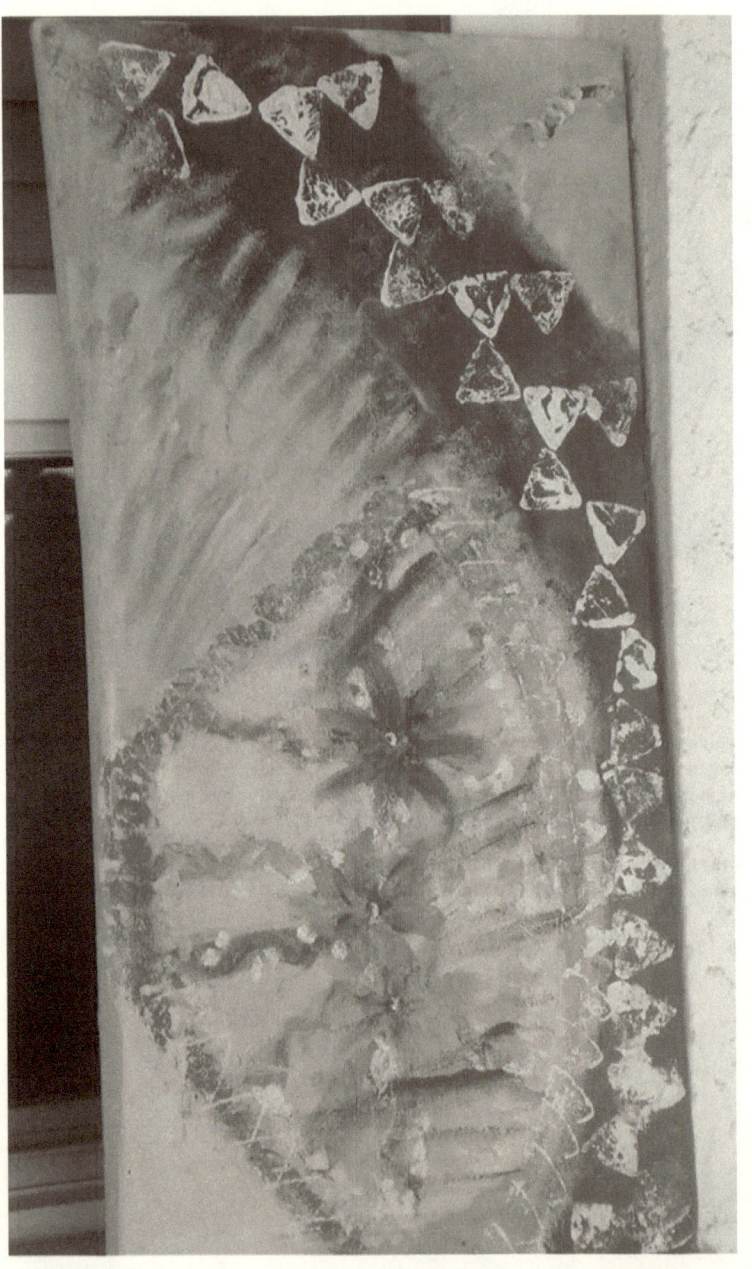

This little angel came about making a woman stand alone in our beauty has a small women she endure multiple eyes, judgement, rejection but in our space world she feel like a beutifull flower in space.

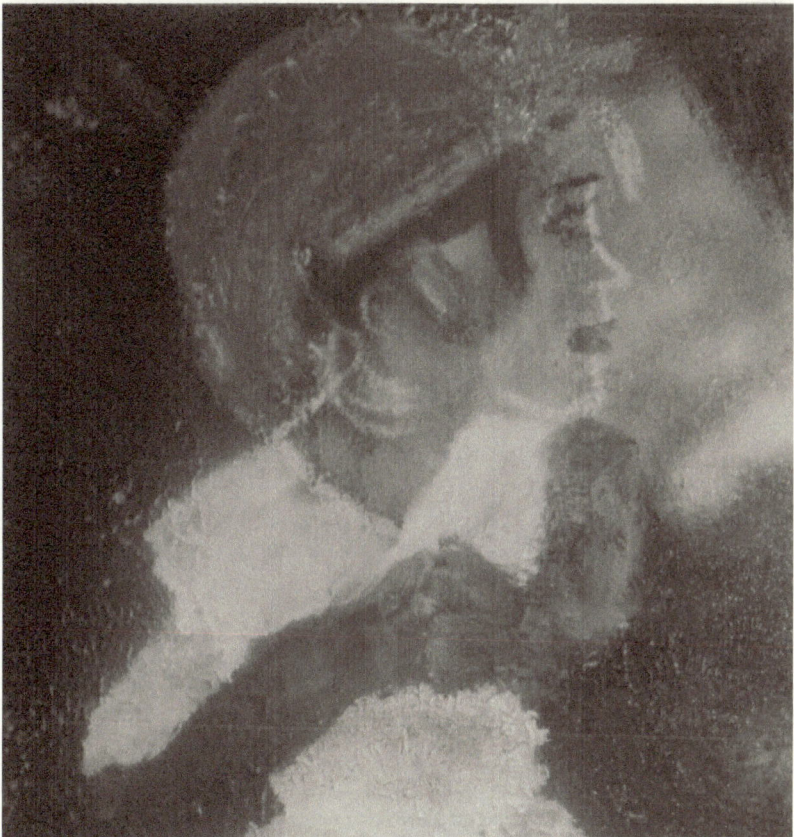

Description:

This is somehting that i felt when seeing this original picture, a lost soul, a free spirit disguise in a junky, a want to be super star, a stone pot head in his total dellusion and despairs.

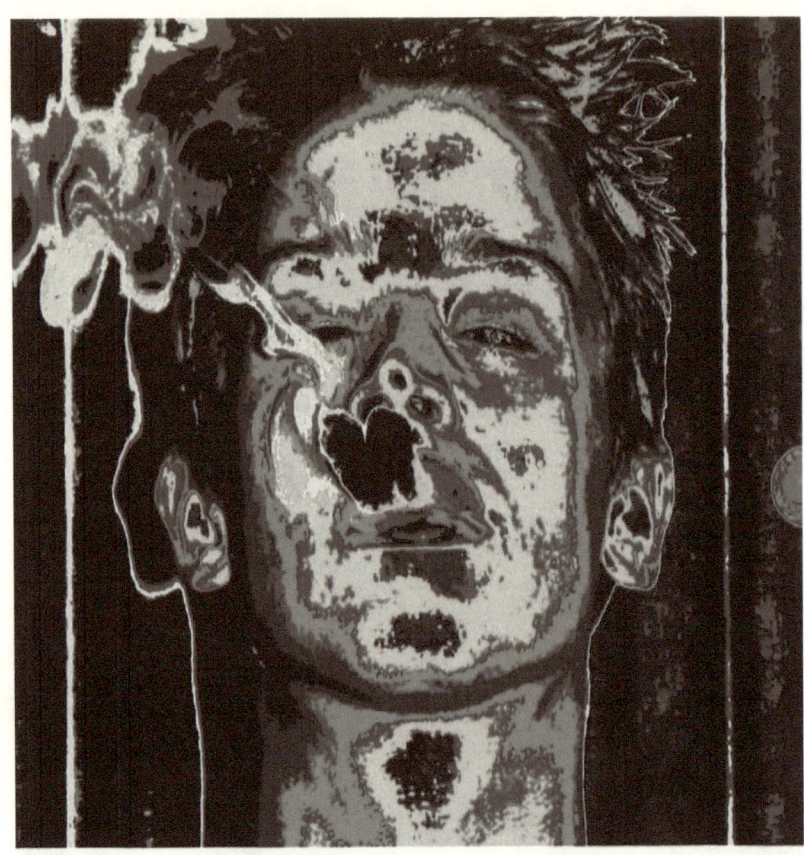

My favorite things to do are cleary the forrest set-up, i have spent so much time walking in deserted forrest trail all alone exploring the nature that even after leaving in the city for a few yearsi can close my eyes and feel this nature crowling under my brushes.

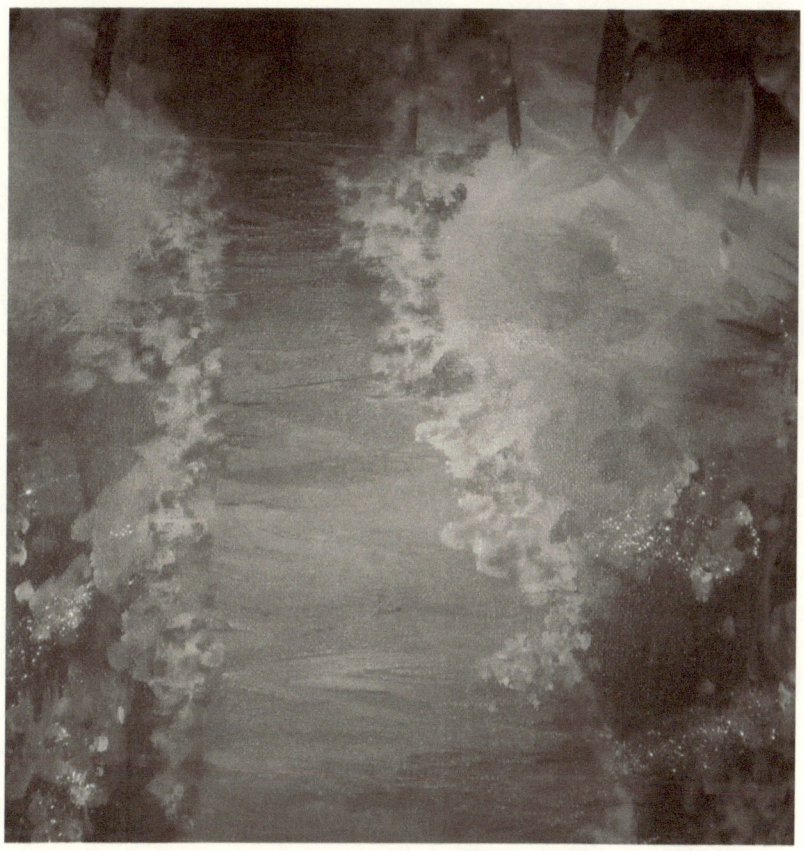

This was a lot of fun to do!!! sometime you just have to try new things without questioning it no matter what is your level of comfort, don't get lost in precision, do what feel good to you!

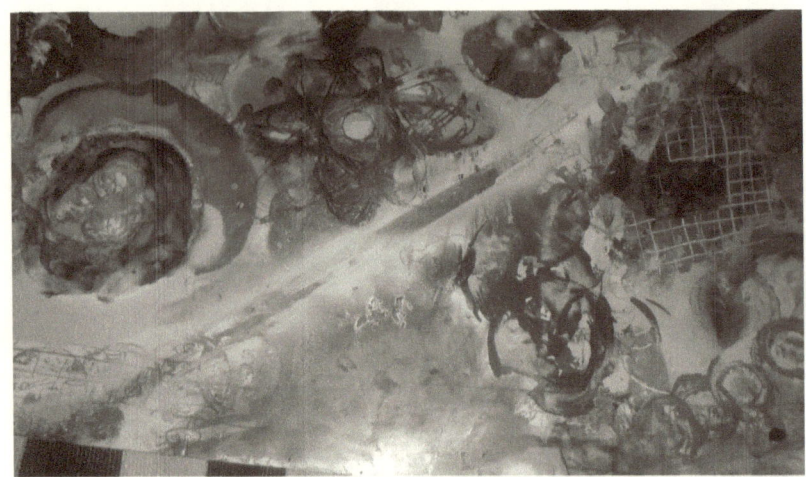

My inspiration of all time!!! I pick this one because aftyer learning about his life and inspiration i felt that what he really wanted to share with others was what he admire and saw everyday.

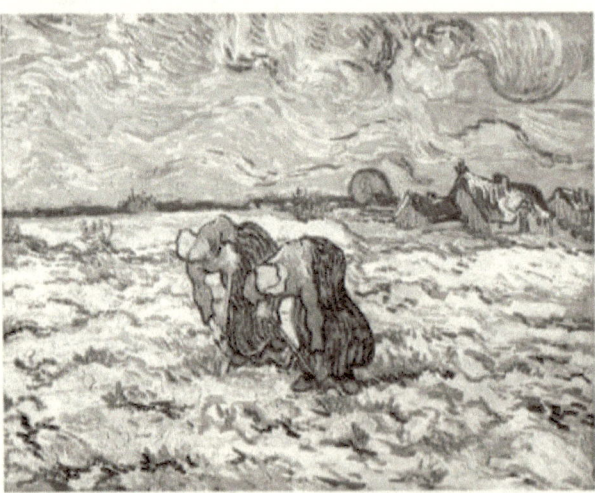

My Co-Artist Visionarist" Michael Baca"

Above is a link to somne of his creation:

https://www.facebook.com/VcreativeArt16/videos/2132532400306865/

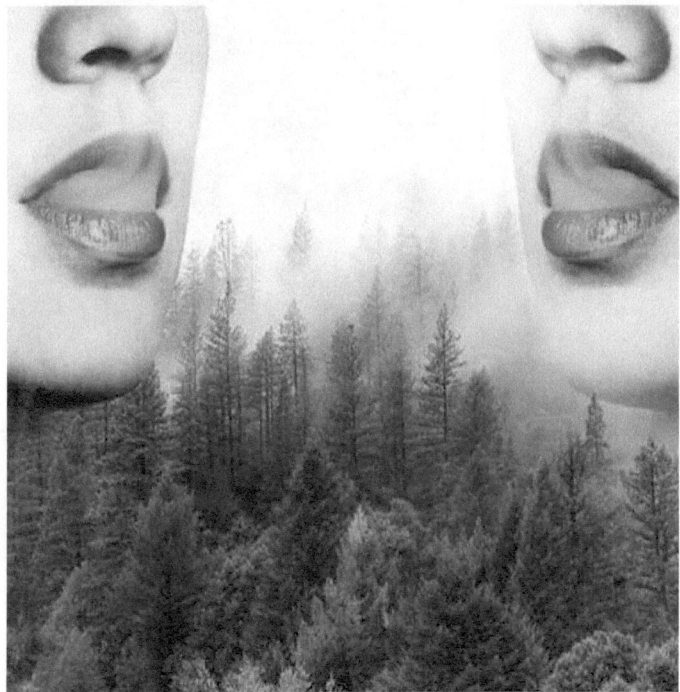

My logo with lighter light in the background.

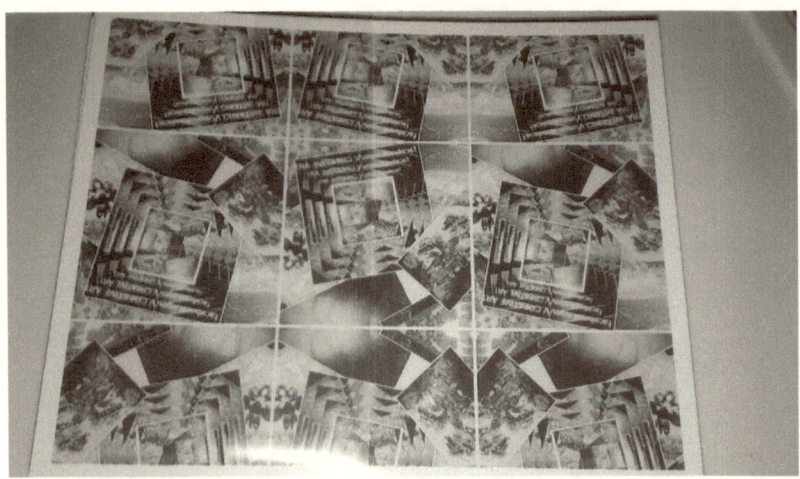

One of Michael Baca visionary digital design creation

I find his work incredible and it connect with this audiences in so many ways

It has a message and story in everything that he does, I personally never get tired of staring at it! It's simply magical!

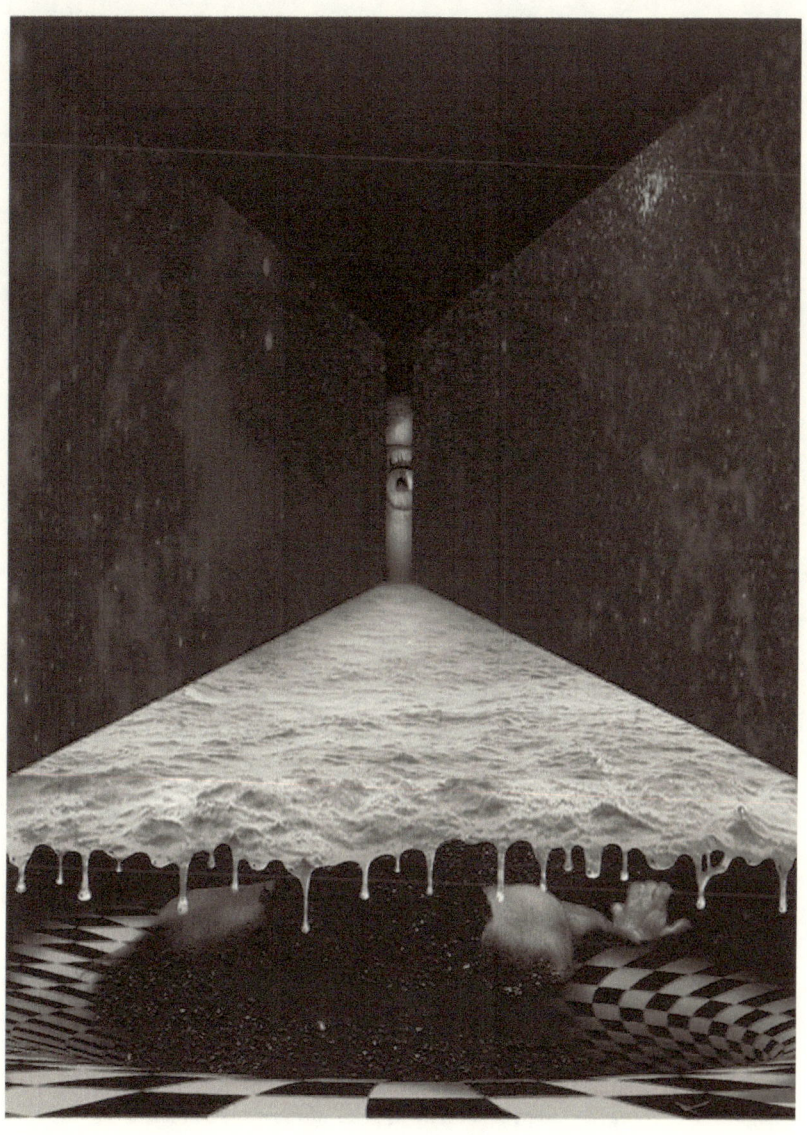

One day i felt like a lost puppie in the modern technology world and mostly in this art world, after following all this social media groups and news articles i decided to read the best material outhere and booost my brain with better knowledge of our new advance progress in marketing technology and art marketing so when i draw this guy in the cover of a marketing startegic magasine i also added this multiple memory capacity space chart that he was indulging for him to be on top of his game.

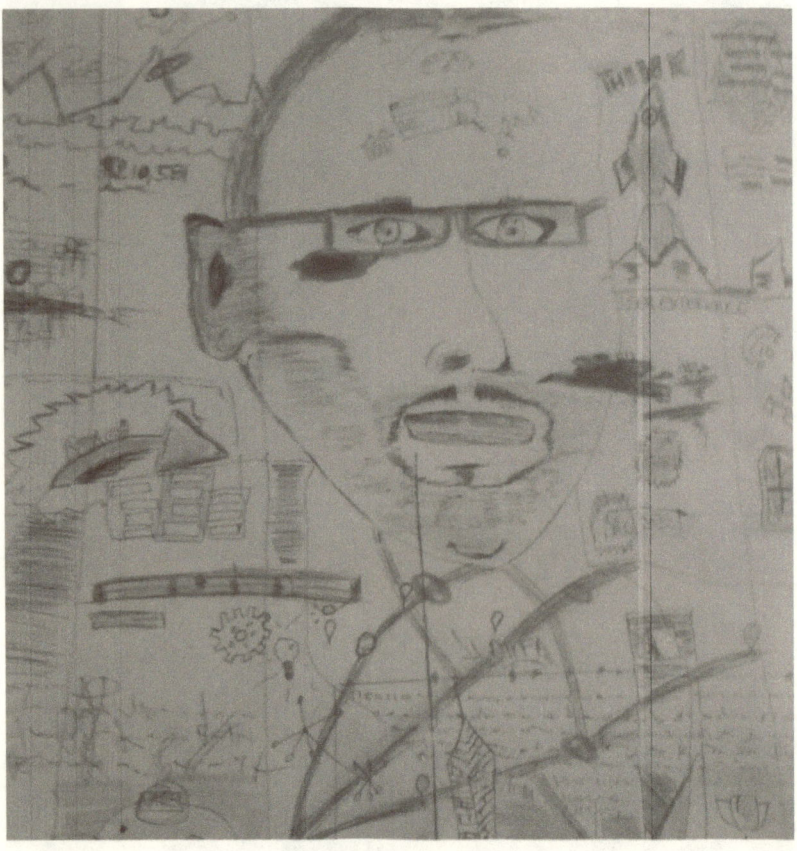

By Michael Baca

I saw this has a eye opener, a tiny window frame place into a infinite universe.

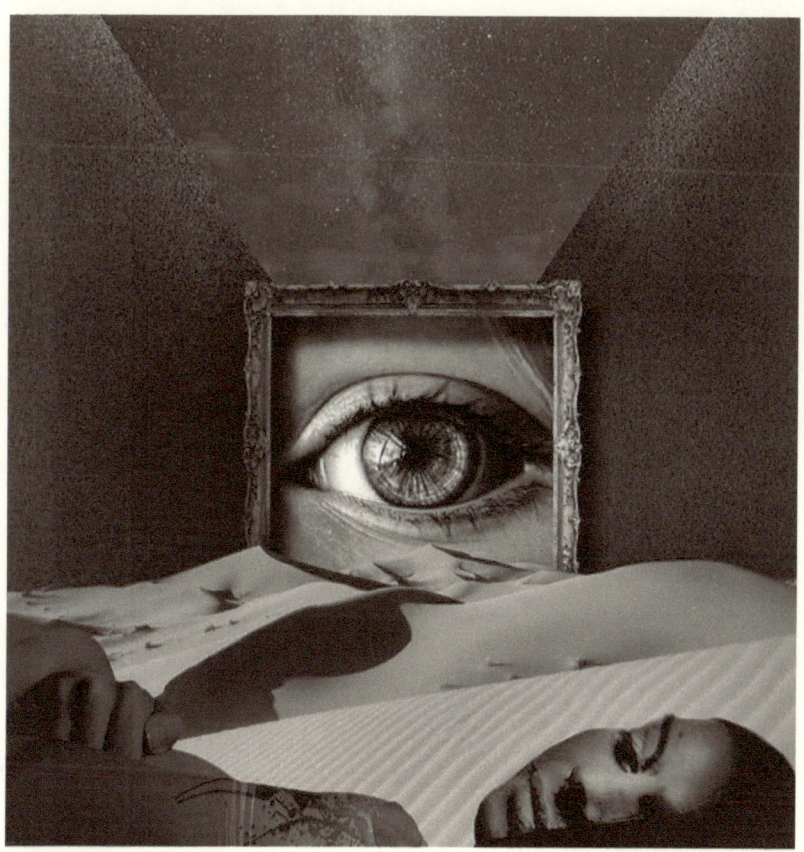

By Michael Baca again! see this time this eyes seem way more open and the picture more colorfull but the red indicate a little bit of pain. you can find him on Facebook @Michaelbaca

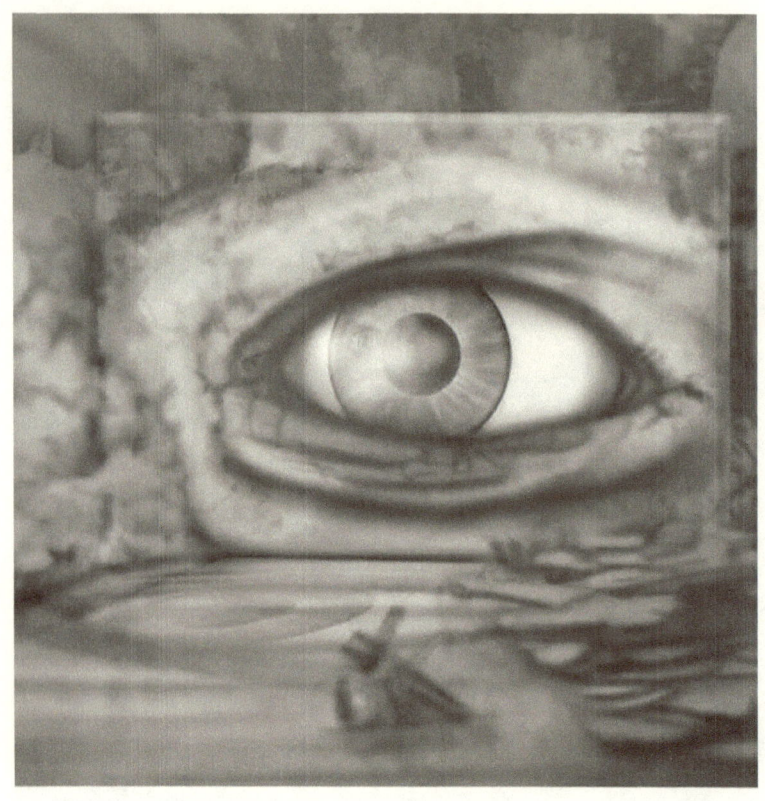

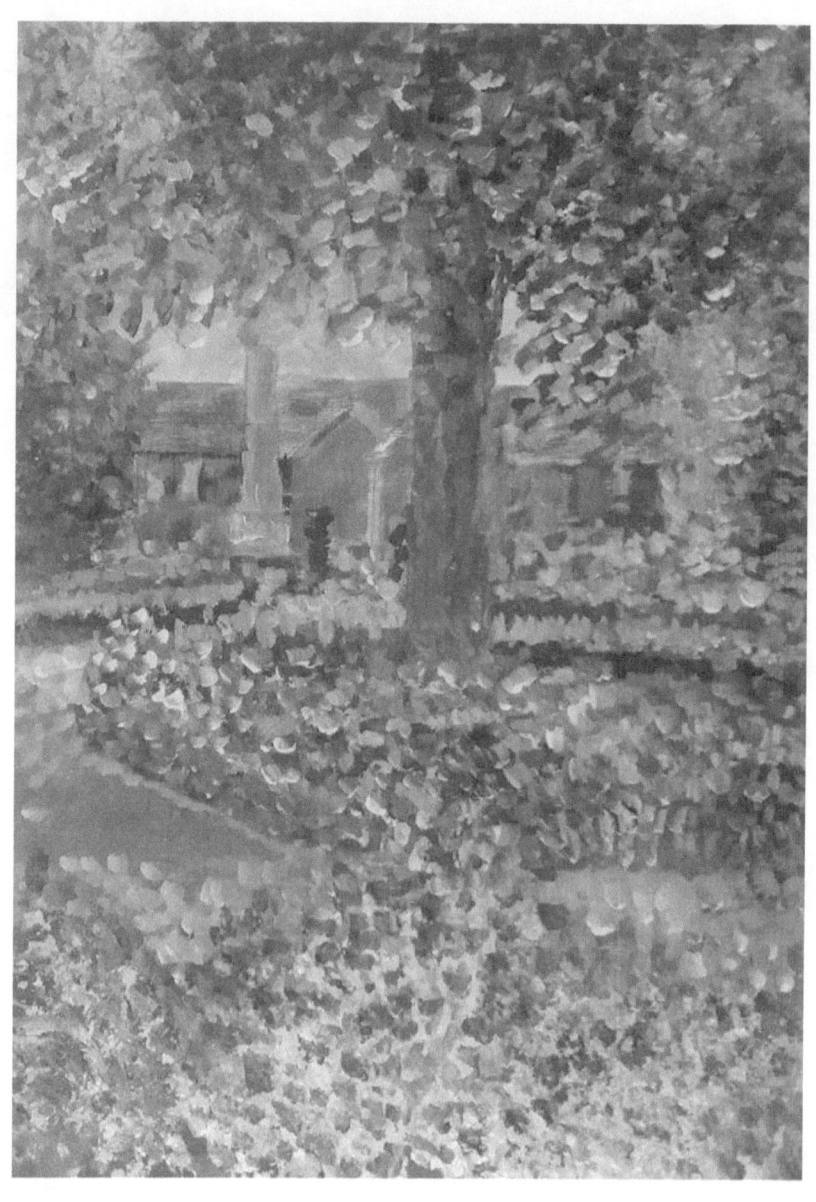

This is a collage of this wonderfull artist who contribuated in this sucess of Vcreativeart16

Michael baca, Kimmy Hutchins, Matthew Evens and R.perry

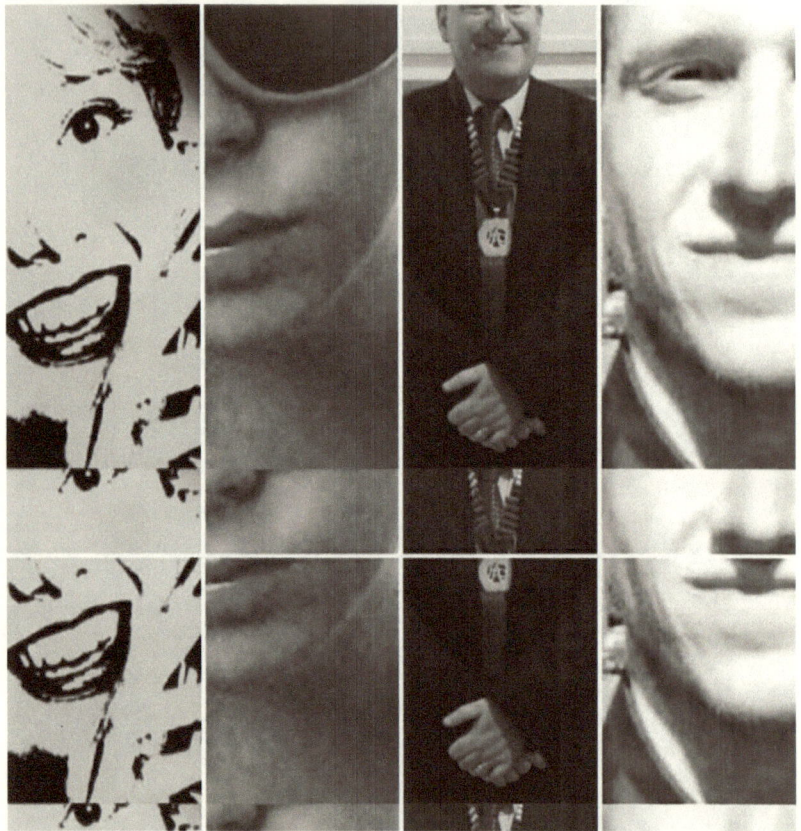

By Mattthew evans

If you want to work on creating persepctive within the sky reach this is the perfect image!

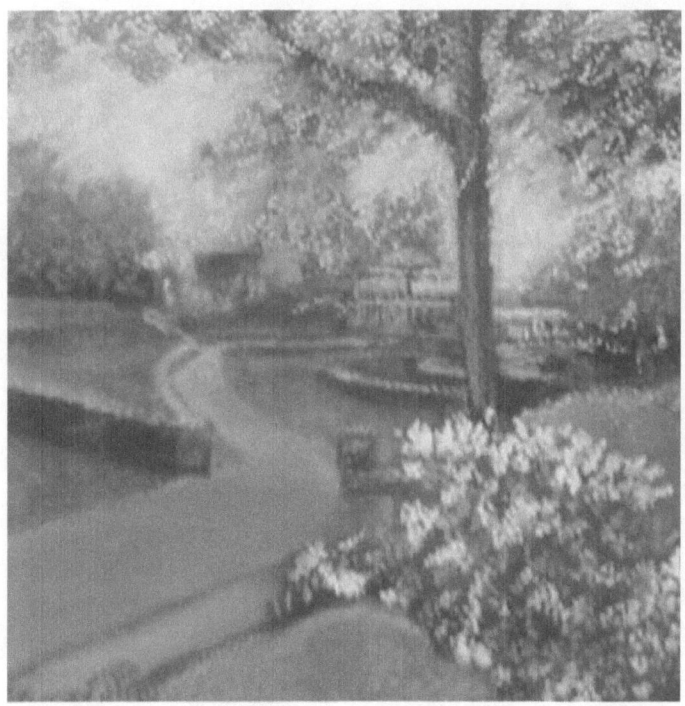

I was feeling like i needed to tell my story somehow so i picture myself thinking into a tiny box and showing the result of my taught into paper with this eye pupil revealing this inspiration.

https://www.facebook.com/VcreativeArt16/videos/2121564784736960/

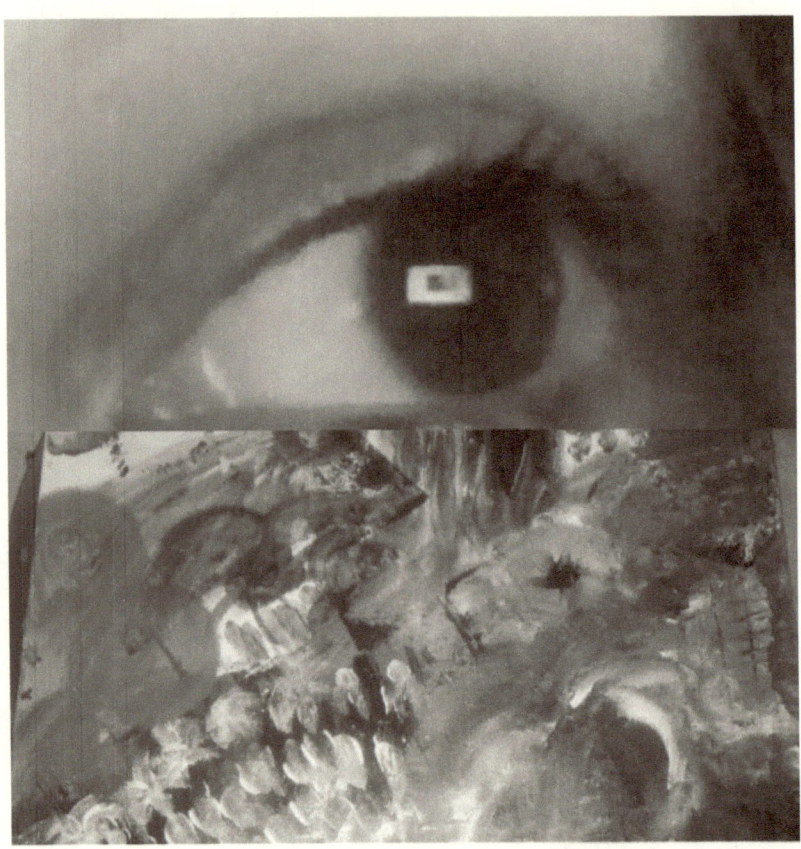

BY Michael Baca

What a treat, please feel free to ask him how he came about to come up with such great ideas and you can also order print and poster on our fineart shopp or showing support by sending donation directly to this artist.

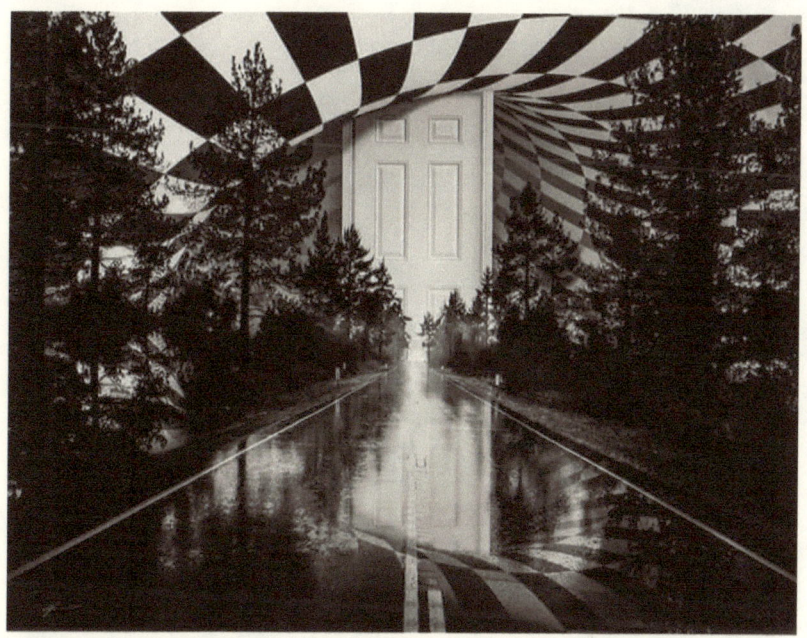

A simple collage i did for father day, these day we have to many app to choose from and sometime it can get seriously confusing i like to keep it simple and modern and stay with our evolution within my owm perception.

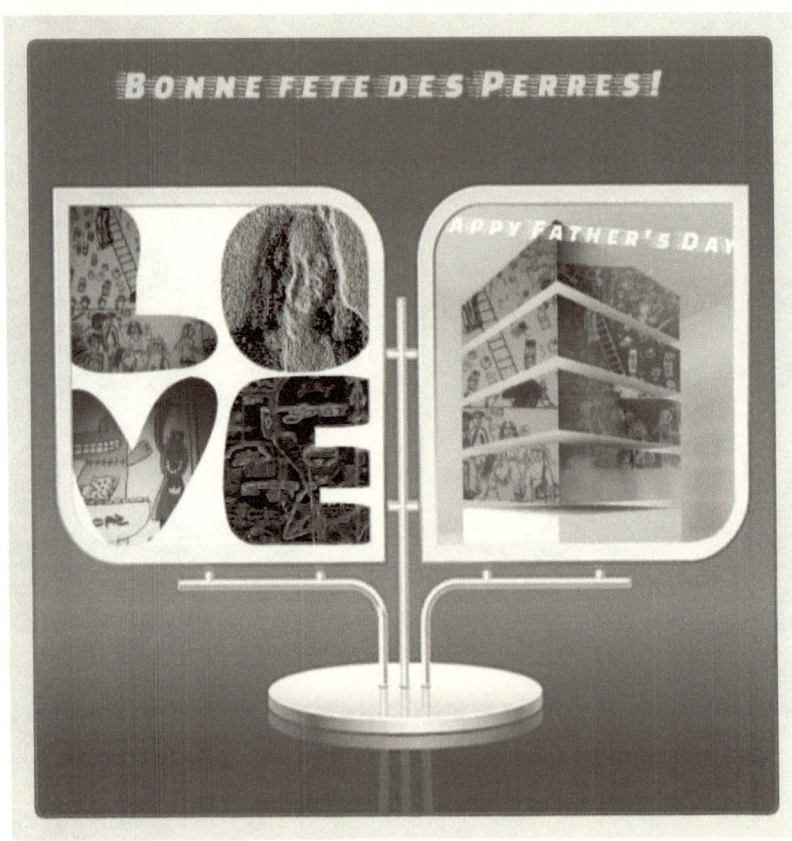

I did this has a idea of exploring the dark sky while fireworks would be blowing in the the sky.

My goal here was to point out the combustion of explosion right on top of this joyfull palmtree.

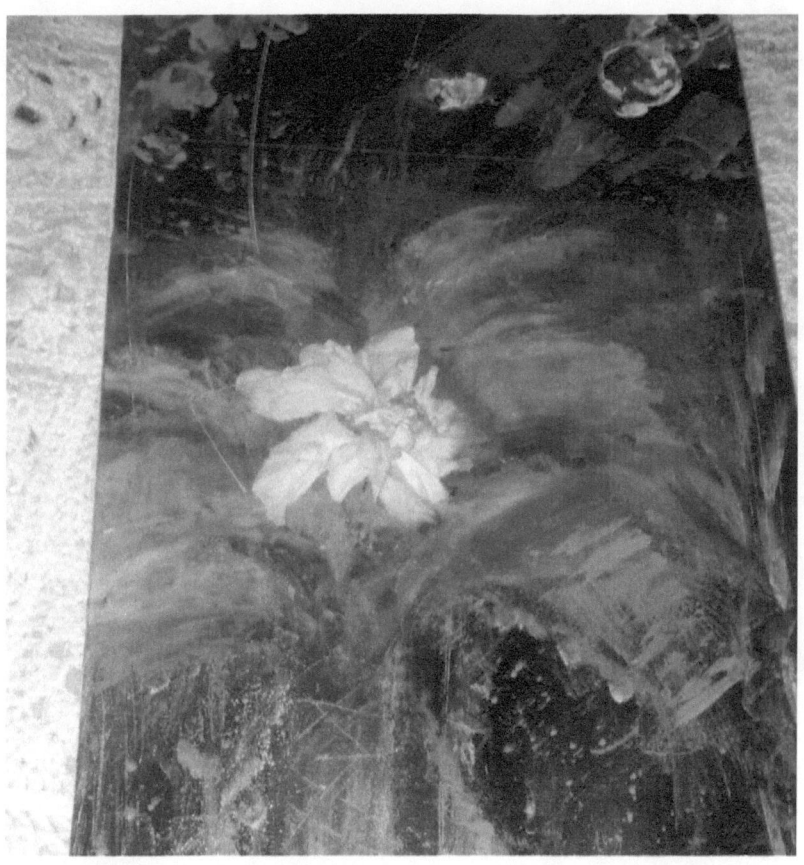

Sunset in Florida capture by a tiny trail. the happy face was intended to bring some lightning into depressing home or people in distress.

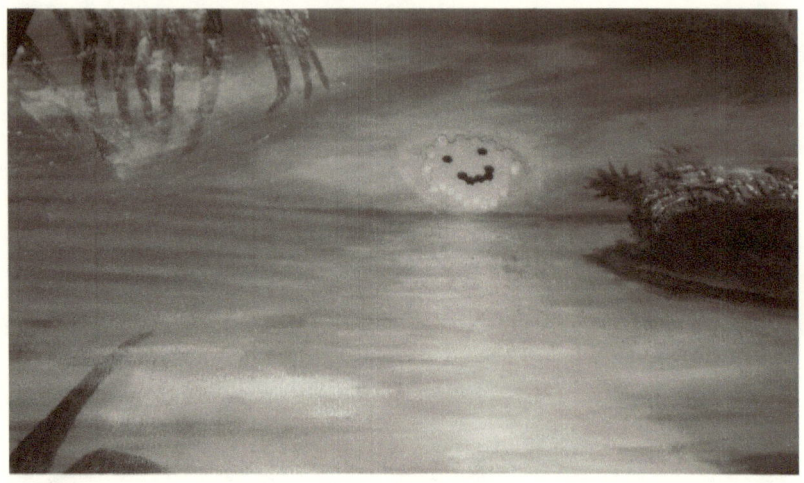

This is much older : I made that in 2006" I really enjoy plaing with color contrast then. this was meant to be some sort of volcano combustion occuring by a deserted island in California

https://www.facebook.com/VcreativeArt16/videos/vl.1779523949024840/2056169041276535/?type=1

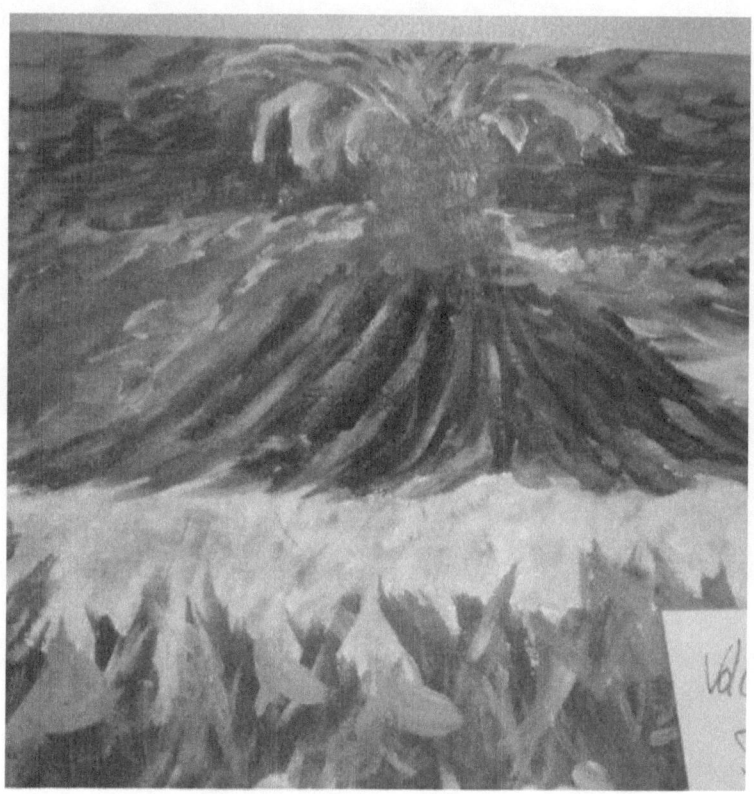

https://www.facebook.com/VcreativeArt16/videos/2145113995715372/ **this link is just to show you how desperate i was for getting my own art studio workshop**

here is this article made by a journalist on artist who their live have been challenging

She ask me to draw somehting who will portray how you felt when feeling alienated by others and this is all i could come up with, it's not pretty because when you leave in distress you don't feel good or pretty, it's uneven because when your unbalance and confuse everything is unstable in your mind. it's scary because when you feel threatned, terrorized, afraid, bullied for no reason you angry at the world, saw the fire represent that anger.

https://l.facebook.com/l.php?u=http%3A%2F%2Ffaceingmentalalillness.heraldtribune.com%2F20
17%2F08%2F11%2Fprofile-trying-to-reconnect-to-her-happy-
childhood%2F&h=ATOa6a3Hc7542b0SpI2E81Va8zdkydUlxzIUsBRy3sCdaidMPEuxnbbnhen8OHr
QUIixxHtQ2CimwkOYpHLLQhzKwvOfxTPVhxLeF30fD09sOEojrYl6FLJWcgSRQ9BEkw0J2fJ_ndpatw
b7xnR7KpvMIus15ClxHHbBUXmmhASA6v6c-

1wuHbQyxO1pwkjn3TfiXQtGHaXxANEbA1nMop22mVTiZzy0eseFPoy377ewHKqlRal8LWNLF3hTi
46D7pUWTRgmloJN3Rn481UHNjoKnVZ3uvDXYM0

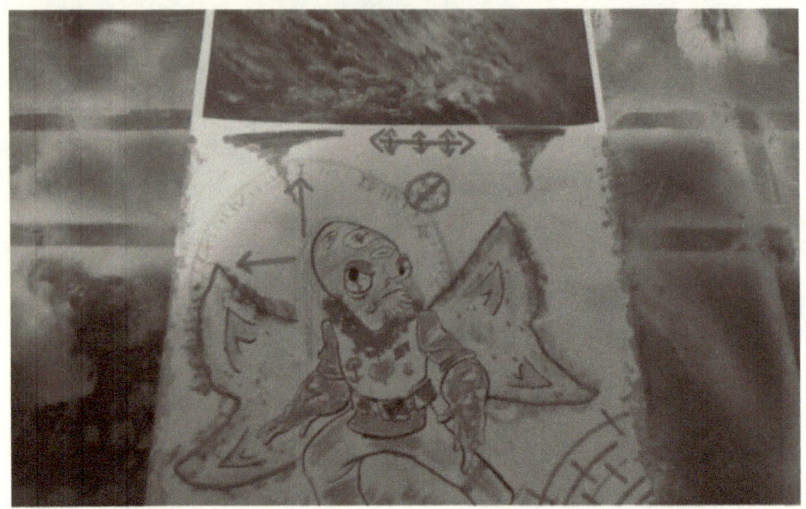

This is a sunset capture!!! no retouch of my City.

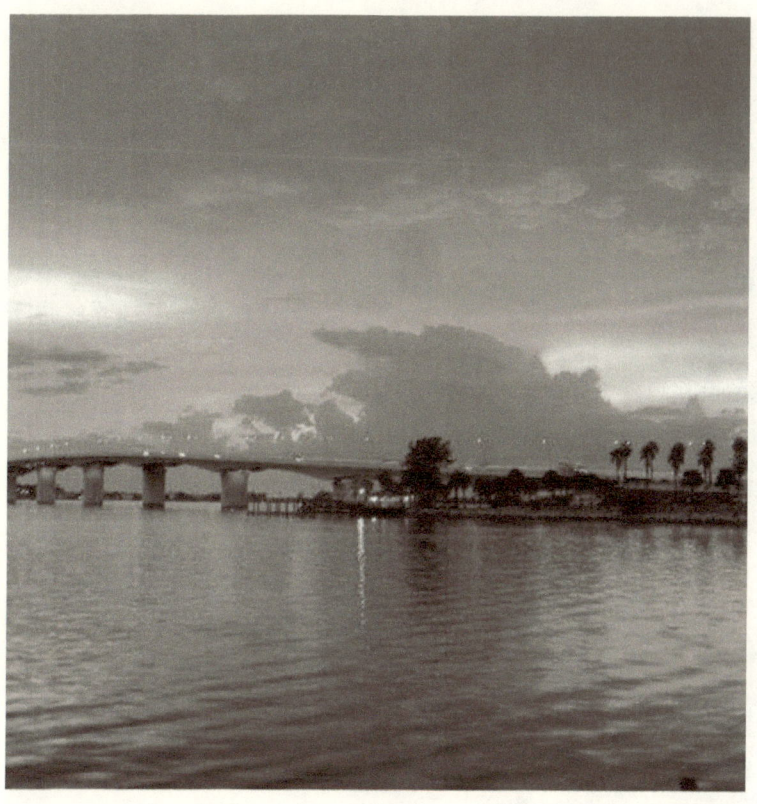

Michael Baca

It seem like he get better everyday!

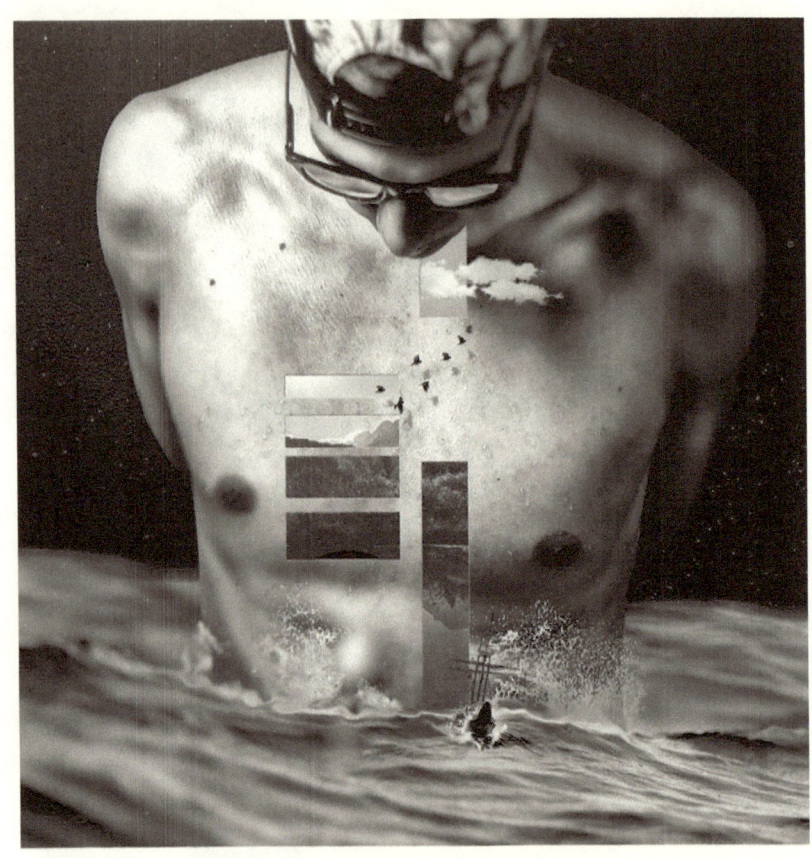

Matthew giant reproduction of one of his award

Here is a link to his profile:

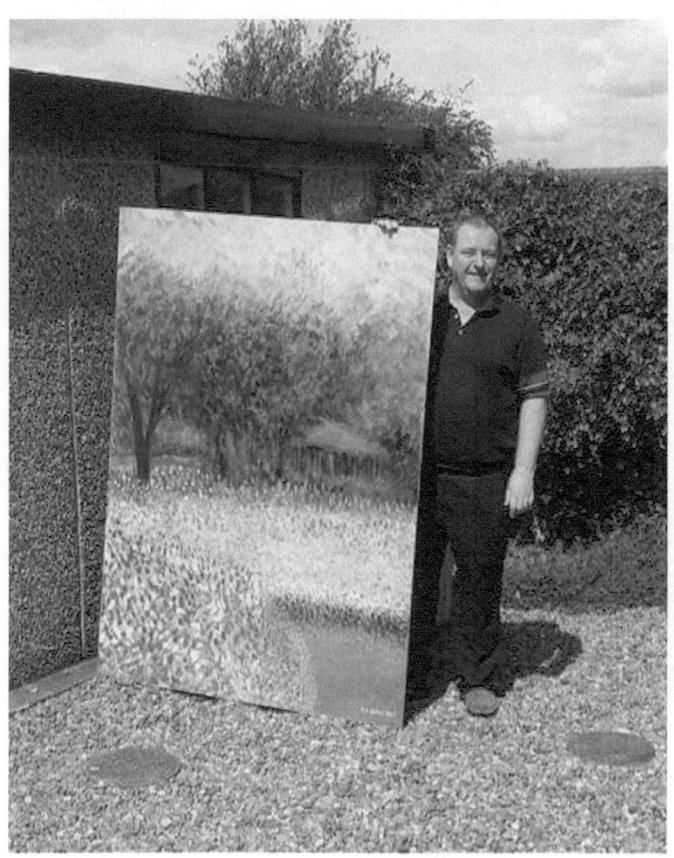

#Vcreativeart16

Instagram @Vcreativeart16

Goggle+ @vcreativeart16

www.facebook.com/vcreativeart16/

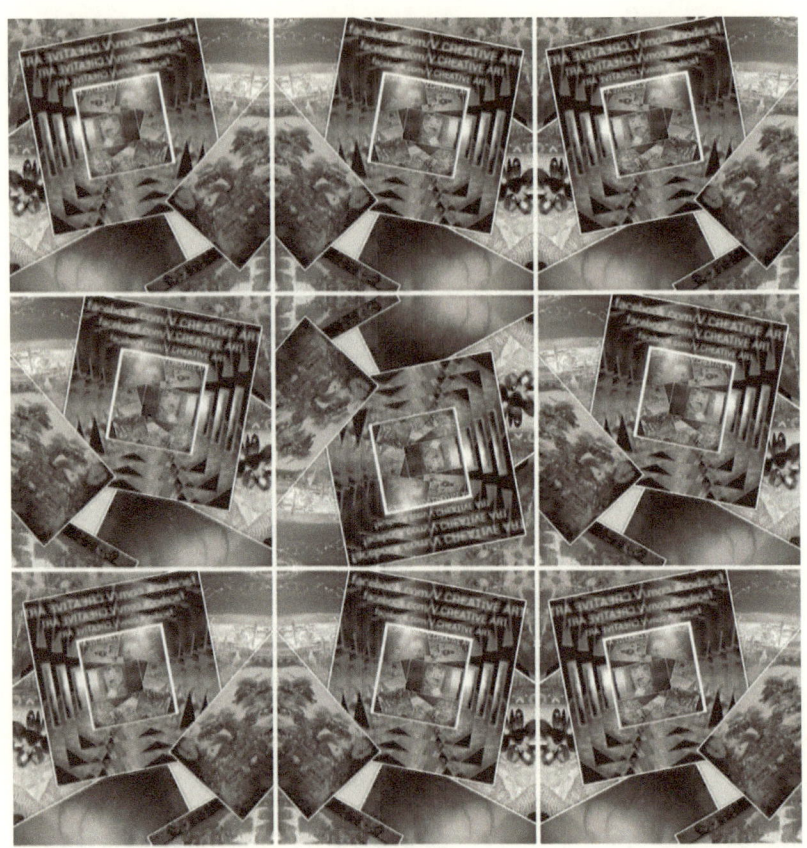

One of my latest creation:

this represent a chineese man whit wisdoom

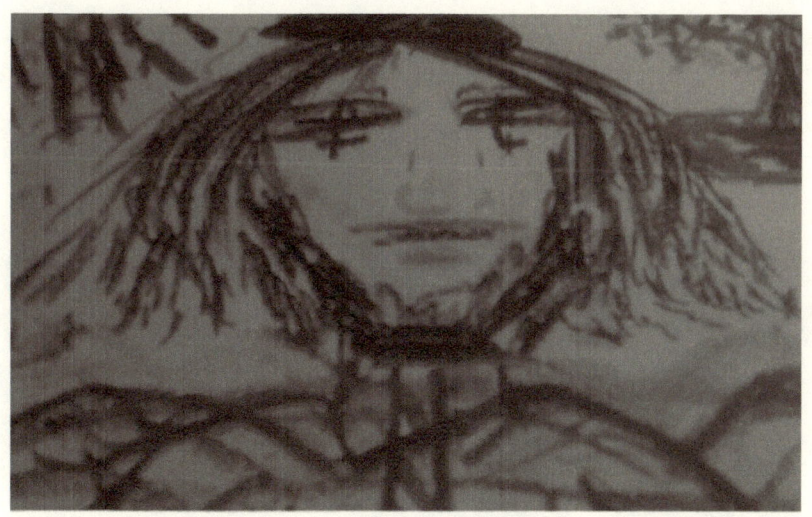

This is my cover for my Meme book

here is the link where you can find it:

https://l.facebook.com/l.php?u=http%3A%2F%2Fa.co%2F5AB1Lcn&h=ATMWHOcSCgVhCjOfA5A
KcyG5vhoTBbpbs0xsUK3lKkivedc7rRcDyfBVMmui5FOWVG6OkVrCb8bbyM_H3yT5qKWSpWMhp
GaLGpCwBiCECKRmq2CxgYfQKHfINbXQcOQIUZUPunnz4RQEE2YfxWwXe7bmMKST4M5yNLdDejc
63eHhcMG3LDkS1oN5b9sdbEZh8PTBpmxc-
rmQBwtlUeitdklrcjx5QnYhSVmMcaGthNHNCvN7R3AE0MwRkytqsj_NypWFVrenKMpOXFY-
rtaScdwaXuUBlbdKE0WU2j1xmw

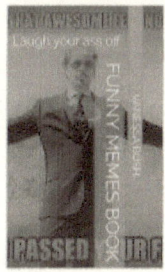

Here are some supportive tools:

Take your time you will not fail!

I do not fail
I succeed in finding out what does not work.

Information on the company:

Group link to the company:

Hypnosis and philosophical influences

https://www.facebook.com/groups/hypnosisbradenton/?ref=group_cover

Veteran PTSD hypnosis therapist

https://www.facebook.com/groups/vcreativeart16hypnosis/

A new day a new story group:

https://www.facebook.com/groups/anewdayanewstory/

Category

Art Gallery, Author, Entertainment, Hypnosis, Artists

Company Name

VCreativeArt16. INC register with

Florida sunbiz has a non-profit INC

Username on Facebook and instagram:

@VcreativeArt16

Always Open/ Online art gallery, located in Manatee county, FL

BUSINESS INFO:

Created in August 2016

My business is a charitable company who offer services to veterans, special needs, MS, cancer patient, special needs and their family.

INTERESTS

Travel, Research, Explore, Aquatic sports, Museums, Writing, Painting.

ADDITIONAL CONTACT INFO

kellybush@live.com

http://www.2-vanessa-bush.pixels.com/

Phone: (941) 524-2883

Director, founder:

Vanessa Bush

Affiliations

Artists:

Michael Baca, Kimmy Hutchins, Matthew evans.

Gallery:

Beautiful disaster photography, Matthew evans seascape gallery, Michael baca (Artist gallery)

About

Versatile group of artists uniting their creative visions to bring unity, peace, cosmic idealism and surrealism influence toward humanity and expression.

Extra information:

Hypnotherapy certification in 2015

Veteran and special needs ceu's from VHA/veteran, 40CME credits with American health association.

Civil rights

Case manager for adult and child training with FCB

Fine art and film production at SFO Art Academy training

Two years of attending at a performing art school in Toulouse, France

Exhibits and shows presentation in manatee county 2015-2017

International competition reward for three years

Poetry and writer award received between 2001-2007

Painting exhibition at Olympian Gallery in Fort Myers in 2012

Publications of nature photography 2003-2009 for local newspaper.

Team member award for customer service in art ventures fundraiser.

lead award for imagination and event planning for University essay project.

Newspaper Articles by the Sarasota Herald published on 08/12/2017

National Swimming competition medal's for 12 years.

Travel and event planning 45 CC

Health and nutrition 65 CC

Thank you for reading this book and i hope it was helpfull for your journey toward being this artist you wanted to be!!!

Please spread the world, visit our group, volunteer, sponsor us, donate or contribute toward our growth by buying through our fineartshopp, facebook shopp, buy our E-book on kindle unlimited, grant our mission to make the world a better place everyday!

Let's engage in defending human rights together and serving this special needs, veterans, cancer patient, Supporting MS, and many other who need us!

Contact information:

kellybush@live.com

(941) 524-2883 LMTC

write us on facebook www.facebook.com/vcreativeart16

Sincerely Yours

Vcreativeart16 Team and Director

With all our love and kindness we wish you the best journey possible!

www.ingramcontent.com/pod-product-compliance
Lightning Source LLC
Chambersburg PA
CBHW021905170526
45157CB00005B/1971